ARGUING ABOUT TASTES

KENNETH J. ARROW LECTURE SERIES

KENNETH J. ARROW LECTURE SERIES

Kenneth J. Arrow's work has so deeply shaped the course of economics for the past sixty years that, in a sense, every modern economist is his student. His ideas, style of research, and breadth of vision have been a model for generations of the boldest, most creative, and most innovative economists. His work has yielded seminal theorems in areas such as general equilibrium theory, social choice theory, and endogenous growth theory, proving that simple ideas have profound effects. The Kenneth J. Arrow Lecture Series highlights economists, from Nobel laureates to groundbreaking younger scholars, whose work builds on Arrow's scholarship as well as his innovative spirit. The books in the series are an expansion of the lectures that are held in Arrow's honor at Columbia University.

The lectures have been supported by Columbia University's Committee on Global Thought, Program for Economic Research, Center on Global Economic Governance, and Initiative for Policy Dialogue.

Discovering Prices: Auction Design in Markets with Complex Constraints, Paul Milgrom
Time and the Generations: Population Ethics for a Diminishing Planet, Patha Dasgupta
Ethical Asset Valuation and the Good Society, Christian Gollier
Creating a Learning Society: A New Approach to Growth, Development, and Social Progress, Reader's Edition, Joseph Stiglitz and Bruce Greenwald
Moral Hazard in Health Insurance, Amy Finkelstein
The Arrow Impossibility Theorem, Eric Maskin and Amartya Sen
Speculation, Trading, and Bubbles, Jose Scheinkman
Creating a Learning Society: A New Approach to Growth, Development, and Social Progress, Joseph Stiglitz and Bruce Greenwald

ARGUING ABOUT TASTES

MODELING HOW CONTEXT AND EXPERIENCE CHANGE ECONOMIC PREFERENCES

DAVID M. KREPS

WITH

ALESSANDRA CASELLA
AND JOSEPH E. STIGLITZ

COLUMBIA UNIVERSITY PRESS | NEW YORK

Columbia University Press
Publishers Since 1893
New York Chichester, West Sussex
cup.columbia.edu

Library of Congress Cataloging-in-Publication Data
Names: Kreps, David M., author. | Casella, Alessandra, author. | Stiglitz, Joseph E., author.
Title: Arguing about tastes : modeling how context and experience change economic preferences / David M. Kreps with Alessandra Casella and Joseph E. Stiglitz
Description: New York : Columbia University Press, [2023] | Series: Kenneth J. Arrow lecture series | Includes bibliographical references and index.
Identifiers: LCCN 2023018173 | ISBN 9780231209908 (hardback) | ISBN 9780231209915 (trade paperback) | ISBN 9780231558174 (ebook)
Subjects: LCSH: Demand (Economic theory) | Utility theory. | Uncertainty. | Game theory. | Microeconomics. | Consumers' preferences.
Classification: LCC HB801 .K728 2023 | DDC 338.5/212—dc23/eng/20230628
LC record available at https://lccn.loc.gov/2023018173

CONTENTS

CONTENTS

PREFACE

Kenneth Arrow and This Book

I am honored to have delivered the Kenneth J. Arrow Lecture at Columbia University and to have contributed this book to the series of Arrow Lecture volumes. In my opinion, Ken was the most important and significant economist of the twentieth century. But, more than that, Ken was in all respects a mensch. Indeed, if I had to find a flaw, it would be that when it came to writing reference letters, Ken could be too kind, finding ways to praise the work of others that didn't really merit praise. Perhaps Ken was worried that his influence

FIGURE 0.1 Kenneth J. Arrow
Source: Courtesy Stanford News Library.

would be too great, and so he chose to send signals that, because of their uniformity, carried no information at all.

Stories about Ken abound, and, if I may, I take this opportunity to relate two that I personally experienced, both having taken place at the old summer seminar series of the IMSSS (Institute for Mathematical Studies in the Social Sciences). For those unfamiliar with these seminars, they took place on the fourth floor of Encina Hall at Stanford University. Nearly always in the audience were Ken, Bob Aumann, Frank Hahn, Eytan Sheshinski, and Robert Wilson. On occasion, a contingent from Berkeley joined; attendees included, at various times, Gerard Debreu, John Harsanyi, Andreu Mas-Colell, and Roy Radner. For a few years, Joe Stiglitz was a regular attendee, as were Sandy Grossman, Mike Spence, David Starrett, and Hayne Leland. Of course, Mordecai Kurz, who organized things, was always in attendance. And this is not the full list; at times, Oliver Hart, Sergiu Hart, John Geanakoplos, and Eric Maskin spent the summer, and (of course) there were many distinguished folks who flowed through to give seminars. It was a spectacular gathering, with Ken always the central figure. (As first a graduate student and then a young assistant professor, I got to observe the proceedings from a seat in the back of the room.)

The first story concerns a seminar given by Franklin Fisher. This was at the time when noncooperative game theory was all the rage in creating models in industrial organization. Frank was unhappy about this surge of "interest" is his domain. He wrote (and later published) a cri de coeur, "Games Economists Play: A Noncooperative View," the main thesis of which is that clever economists can use game theory to get any conclusion they wish, hence these models prove nothing. To illustrate the inanity of using game theory, he recounted how, in a practical question of whether a merger should be allowed to occur, a famous economist—he wouldn't say who, so as not to embarrass—offered testimony that involved the computation of consumer surplus from the three-firm and four-firm Cournot equilibria, asserting that the difference was a good measure of the cost to consumers of the merger if it were allowed to take place. Obviously, Fisher opined, this was simply silly.

And later in Fisher's talk, Ken related that he (Ken) had been the famous economist in question, and he provided his rationale. Of course, the audience was composed primarily of theorists. But it seemed to me from the back of the room that Ken had convinced the audience that this was manifestly the right computation to have used.

The second story needs a bit of a setup. Ken had a routine at these seminars: He would sit in the same seat at the front, sometimes arriving a few minutes late with his mail. While the speaker began the presentation, Ken would quietly go through his mail. When done with the mail, he would engage in his trademark pencil flip: without looking, he would flip a pencil up in the air and catch it after a full rotation or perhaps two. And then he would often seem to doze off.

At one seminar—I won't identify the speaker—Ken followed this pattern. These seminars ran for nearly 2 hours and had a 15-minute break after an hour for coffee or tea and cookies. And this day (as was often the case), Ken, stimulated by the coffee, was wide awake for the second half. A question was asked of the speaker, which Ken promptly began to answer.

The speaker objected with approximately the following words: "Professor Arrow: I know that you are smarter than me, but you've thought about this topic for an hour or so while I've thought about it for months and months. So perhaps you should let me answer the question. I think I'm in a better position to do so."

To which Frank Hahn immediately responded, "My dear young man"—Frank used a different term than "man," but I don't think I should say which—"you are so confused."

And Ken proceeded with his response to the question, which showed that notwithstanding his seeming lack of attention in the first hour, he understood perfectly the topic of the seminar, perhaps even better than did the speaker. The story is told of a famous mathematician (Erdös?), who had his students read to him the titles of published papers, following which he would provide the incorporated theorems and their proofs. When it came to papers in economics, my impression was that Ken could do this, and it was only his gentle nature that prevented him from doing so.

When I was invited to give the talk on which this book is based, Prof. Stiglitz suggested that it is traditional to tie the talk to some topic to which Ken contributed. This essay is about behavior and, in particular, dynamic behavior by individuals in settings of "social exchange." Arrow's coherence axiom is the basic formal building block in revealed-preference theory, so that's something of a connection. A more substantial connection is to Arrow's paper "Gifts and Exchanges" in *Philosophy and Public Affairs*.[1] According to Google Scholar (as of October 28, 2021), this paper has around 3,000 citations.

It ought to be 30,000; if you haven't read this paper, which anticipates much of what follows in this essay, you should.[2] However, in "Gifts and Exchanges," Ken does not attempt to build formal (mathematical) models of the important ideas he discusses. And, to my mind, perhaps Ken's greatest contribution to economics is that he set the standard for taking somewhat vague ideas and expositing them in the formal language of (mathematical) models, permitting better understanding of the ideas and exposing their strengths and weaknesses. I don't reach Ken's standard in this regard. But in terms of aspiration, that's what I'm trying to do.

This book collects a bunch of ideas and drafts of papers that I've played with over the years.[3] There is little here that is original to me; the axiomatization of internalization in the appendix might count as original, but, if so, it is not very profound. Instead of presenting original work, my objective is to pull together a collection of ideas that link the economics of relationships with social psychology and to give these ideas a nontraditional (for economics) dynamic spin. Having taught human resource management and written both a textbook and a trade book on the subject, I firmly believe that economics and economists must come to grips with these ideas.[4] Some economists have done so; I provide some references in the text. But these ideas are not (yet) accepted by the mainstream. Hence, this book is an extended polemic: I hope to increase the acceptance of these ideas and spur further work in these directions.

I am indebted to many individuals for helpful conversations over the years and, more recently, both for conversations that helped me better to understand how psychologists view these issues and for comments on the manuscript. With apologies to anyone I've missed and absolving all from ideas and concepts that I inevitably have failed to grasp, I thank Mohammad Akbapour, James Baron, Sam Bowles, Alessandra Casella, Bob Gibbons, Linda Ginzel, Deborah Gruenfeld, Bengt Holmstrom, Tamar Kreps, Edward Lazear, Dale Miller, Suresh Naidu, Paul Oyer, John Roberts, José Scheinkman, Joel Sobel, Joseph Stiglitz, and two anonymous reviewers. The financial support of the Chi-fu Huang and Marina Chen Charitable Trust is gratefully acknowledged.

I am also grateful to several folks at Columbia and Columbia University Press: First and foremost is Joe Stiglitz, both for the opportunity to give the Arrow Lecture and for his encouragement for the topic and for the book as it developed. I also am grateful to acquisition editor Christian Winting and and designer Elliott Cairns, and to KGL's editorial services manager Ben Kolstad and copyeditor Chris Curioli.

It would normally be appropriate to dedicate this work to the memory of Ken Arrow. I dedicated my book *Microeconomic Foundations I* to Ken, and he certainly is worthy of two dedications from me. But instead, I'll dedicate this to the memory of a treasured colleague, Eddie Lazear (who would probably hate what I write here).

ARGUING ABOUT TASTES

INTRODUCTION

Gary Becker on Prenups

Gary Becker once wrote a periodic column for *Business Week*, and, in the December 29, 1997, issue, his column was titled "Why Every Married Couple Should Sign a Contract."[1] Becker argues, roughly, that marriage, a complex contractual arrangement (subject to dissolution), should be fine-tuned to the circumstances and desires of the two parties. In some cases and cultures, prenuptial agreements are the norm. But in the United States at least, the overwhelming majority of cases are governed by a one-size-fits-all divorce law, as interpreted somewhat arbitrarily by a family-court judge. Better, Becker argues, to take matters into your own hands and craft a detailed agreement best suited to you and your partner. And to deal with the objection that one party might take the mention by the other of such an arrangement as a signal of . . . something less than complete romantic love at the outset, Becker says that making such an arrangement mandatory will defeat this signaling problem.

Because inferences drawn upon the receipt of out-of-equilibrium signals are hard to control, Becker's conjecture—

that making these contracts mandatory will solve the signaling problem—can be questioned. What if the social equilibrium is that, required by law to have a prenup, the common practice is to resort to some one-size-fits-all, simple boilerplate contract? Indeed, in Jewish law, a contract, called the Ketubah, is required. But, at least when I was married, a nicely preprinted Ketubah was presented to me (and the father of the bride, with whom this contract is made), very much a form document. In such a case, one can imagine that expressing a desire not to use the standard boilerplate document would be "out-of-equilibrium" and taken as a signal of . . . something untoward.

From the perspective of orthodox economics, Becker's argument is surely correct, if we believe his contention that making such contracts mandatory defeats the signaling problem. Economists think of individual behavior as being driven by tastes (or preferences), beliefs, and the circumstances in which one finds oneself. If fine-tuning those circumstances does not adversely affect tastes or beliefs, then, certainly, fine-tuning to suit those fixed tastes and beliefs can only help. I don't believe that Becker's "make-contracts-mandatory fix" for the problem of adverse implications arising from a fine-tuning exercise necessarily works. But suppose it did. In orthodox economics, each individual's preferences are fixed and unchanging characteristics of the individual. Granting this premise of orthodox economics, Becker is on sound logical grounds.

But is this premise—that negotiating and, even more to the point, executing a prenup will have no impact on preferences—reasonable? When I first was thinking about this question, I asked various psychologist and sociologist colleagues what they thought of Becker's argument. All of them worried about what such an arrangement would do to the attitudes (a term psychologists seem to like more than "preferences") of the happy couple. Phrases like "this will objectify the relationship" were offered, meaning that the existence of a negotiated contract would turn a relationship based on love into a contractual relationship, to the detriment of both parties. In a loving relationship, each member of the loving couple has strong intrinsic motivation to sacrifice their personal short-run interests if there is enough benefit for their partner. "Intrinsic motivation" here is psychology speak for "they do it because they prefer to do it, even if there are no future consequences from doing so, even if it is done 'in the dark.' " Impose a contract, and each partner, now a contractee, sees their responsibility to be living up to the terms of the contract and no more.

Becker, in his essay, focuses on a formal, legal agreement between prospective partners, aimed primarily at the terms by which the marriage can be dissolved. Quoting him: "Contracts permit [couples] entering into marriage to make divorce a difficult option by limiting their breakup to desertion and other extreme circumstances. They make a long-term commitment to each other more secure. People won't have to worry that their relationship could be easily abrogated when they have financial or health problems or when one of them tires of the other or meets someone else" (fourth paragraph of the *Hoover Digest* reprint).

A legal arrangement raises questions, in the spirit of Oliver Williamson, of ex post transaction costs.[2] In the fantasy world of orthodox economics, all contingencies are efficiently provided for ex ante, and contracts are costlessly enforced. In the real world, unforeseen contingencies do arise, and enforcement of legal arrangements can be costly. As the couple faces contingencies unforeseen at the time of their marriage, will they (jointly) wish to adapt their arrangement? To do so may involve significant or even prohibitive legal costs. And there are enforcement costs; even if the pair has executed a legal agreement, what will it cost one side to go to court to enforce the terms of the agreement?

These considerations are worth pondering, but they are not my point. I wonder whether the existence of a legal contract—even if it covers every contingency and can be costlessly enforced—changes the attitudes of the partners concerning their "obligations" to one another.

An anonymous reviewer observes that Becker's reliance on legally binding contracts raises a further and much more subtle question: When it comes to mundane tasks, such as shopping for food or cleaning the bathroom, what about less formal ex ante agreements between the two parties? Certainly, the cost of renegotiating such informal agreements is, one expects, significantly less than the renegotiation costs of a legal contract. Adaptability to new and unforeseen contingencies is presumably easier. Self-enforcement in the manner of relational contracts ("If you don't clean the bathroom, I'm not going to do the dishes in a timely manner") is feasible. And clarity on these points—when the bathroom needs cleaning, who is responsible?—will reduce subsequent frictions. On the other hand, fixing these things in advance does to some extent objectify the relationship: "I did the dishes as prescribed by our agreement; that's the deal we made. You are responsible for the bathroom, notwithstanding unanticipated work that you had to bring home." That there are trade-offs here is, I think, indisputable. The point of this book is to promote recognition of half the trade-off: the half that fixing responsibilities can objectify the relationship to the detriment of the relationship's long-term health.

In a narrow sense, this book explores why I think Becker is giving bad advice. But in a broader sense, the book is an extended polemic against the principle of orthodox economics that *de gustibus non est disputandum*, "there is no arguing about tastes." The principle *de gustibus* is that, however an individual's preferences are formed, economists should take them as given and not worry about how they are formed. Moreover, orthodox economics holds that it is improper to think that preferences can be affected by social context or that they can evolve on the basis of an individual's experiences.[3]

These two ideas—concerning the effect of context on immediate preferences and the evolution of preferences because of experiences—are hardly new to social psychologists or moral philosophers. An example from the field of social psychology is Bem's self-perception theory (discussed at length later in this book).[4] As for philosophers, Sandel discusses the impact of pervasive markets on individual morality.[5]

And these ideas are not new to the literature of economics. The abstract to Henry Aaron's "Distinguished Lecture on Economics in Government," given more than a quarter-century ago, includes the following: "Economists should pay more attention to value formation in economic analysis. First, preferences are not stable in any operationally meaningful way. . . . Second, the economist's model of human psychology is inaccurate and misleading."[6] And at least a few distinguished economists have explored the formation of values/attitudes/preferences.[7] This comes to a half century of such thinking and writing, and the references provided in Note 7 constitute a partial selection of work along these lines.

Nonetheless, the adjective "heterodox" continues to apply to such work because mainstream, orthodox economists and economics hold fast to the principle *de gustibus*. It is purely anecdotal, but a distinguished colleague of mine, on hearing the topic and thesis of my Arrow Lecture, suggested that, insofar as I succeed in convincing others to reject *de gustibus*, it would ruin economics.

That's a heavy charge. But it is one I am prepared to endure. In my teaching life, I have taught microeconomics to professional-degree students, executives, and PhD students and human resource management (HRM) to the first two groups. I have authored or coauthored two books on HRM.[8] And in the context of workplace motivation, I have found economics that adheres to *de gustibus* to be inadequate at least and, too often, downright misleading. In these books and in my teaching, I have hedged; I have held that traditional economics (or more accurately, the nearly traditional economics of Oliver Williamson) and social and cognitive psychology offer different and complementary perspectives. Practitioners trying to manage human resources effectively must keep both perspectives in mind. However, I have come to believe that a fusion of these approaches—in particular, a fusion that involves economists incorporating "changing preferences" in a serious way in their models and analysis—should be high on the agenda of economics.

Hence, I write this book (and previously I gave the talk on which it is based). There is very little here that is original to me. (Perhaps the axiomatic model of specific-other-regarding preferences in chapter 3 and the appendix is new. If so, it is not significant.) But by presenting a combination of simple formal models, a bit of survey data, and some anecdotes, I hope to do my bit in convincing mainstream economists that it is time to embrace the idea that arguing about tastes—how they are influenced by context and how they evolve—should be an important part of economic modeling and analysis.

This book is largely limited to a discussion of the interaction between intrinsic motivation and extrinsic incentives, both in static situations and in more dynamic contexts. But to be clear, issues about preference formation and evolution are much broader than this. While the focus here is limited, I hope that this limited discussion inspires economists to think more broadly about such things.

The book is organized as follows. chapters 1 through 7 present (almost entirely verbally) some basic ideas concerning how economists and social psychologists model choice and preferences, both statically and dynamically. These basic ideas—a better description is that they are elements of my overall story—are the following:

- The basic principle of *de gustibus* (chapter 1) or the orthodox economist's model of individual choice
- Fitting intrinsic motivation into orthodox economics (chapter 2)

- Modeling formally the idea that one person internalizes the welfare of a specific other person (chapter 3)
- A brief review of three books by economists that break with the traditional view of *de gustibus* (chapter 4)
- Choice and preference in dynamic-choice contexts: the orthodox story, and why it is suspect (chapter 5)
- Some social psychological theories of how context and experience can affect tastes (chapter 6)

Chapter 7 concerns the meme that *extrinsic incentives may drive out intrinsic motivation* and uses the famous debate in the United Kingdom over payment for blood donations (Richard Titmuss vs. agency theory) as the starting point, but going on the orthodox attempts by economists, in particular Bénabou and Tirole, to rationalize this phenomenon.[9]

With the minor exception of chapter 3, all exposition up to the end of chapter 7 is "verbal theorizing." Modern (orthodox) economists by and large prefer formal models of things, so in chapters 8, 9, and 10 I provide some very simple formal models of the power of intrinsic motivation vis-à-vis extrinsic incentives. The bottom line is that intrinsic motivation is powerful because it is free while extrinsic financial incentives come out of someone's pocket.[10] Hence, and insofar as the imposition of extrinsic incentives chills intrinsic motivation, trading off intrinsic motivation for extrinsic incentives can be ineffective and, quite quickly, counterproductive:

- Chapter 8 provides two basic formal models
- Chapter 9 extends those models to a "multitasking" environment

- And in chapter 10, the question is: What if the agent's intrinsic motivation is not aligned with the principal's wishes?

Among the variety of intrinsic motivations that an agent (or the partner in a relationship) might exhibit is internalization of the welfare of the principal (or relationship partner). Subject to some caveats, this type of intrinsic motivation is particularly valuable because it both "solves" the alignment-of-interests problems of chapter 10 and permits trading (more) favors within relationships that would otherwise go undone. These ideas are developed in chapter 11.

The formal models and discussion through chapter 11 are all based on the *static* story that context affects preferences. I contend that identity-economics forces become more powerful and important in dynamic contexts. Chapter 12 introduces dynamics into the story, drawing in particular on Bem's self-perception theory.

To reiterate, the point of this small book is to argue that economists should "worry about tastes." There are serious arguments against this position, and in chapter 13 I first provide some of those arguments and then try to refute them.

The comments of Professors Stiglitz and Casella, offered at the talk on which this book is based, follow, with a brief rejoinder from me.

1

DE GUSTIBUS NON EST DISPUTANDUM

The Mainstream Economic Account of Individual Behavior

In mainstream economics, individual behavior is modeled as maximization subject to constraint. The constraints facing the individual determine her options; her objective function—what she maximizes—is determined by her *tastes* and her *beliefs*. Beliefs concern contingencies (or "states of nature") that will affect her eventual outcome and are typically expressed by a probability distribution over the possible resolutions of those factors; tastes concern her relative evaluation of the outcome once the outcome is determined.

The economic individual—call her *Homo economicus* (or HE)—is assumed to apply careful reason in determining her beliefs. She consults whatever information she has or can access about her environment, together with her prior assessment, then flawlessly applies Bayes rule. Insofar as the actions of other economic actors affect the outcome for her, she makes assessments about their actions. It has become common in economic modeling to employ noncooperative game theory and, in particular, equilibrium analysis (Nash equilibrium plus refinements) to say which assessments are reasonable for her to make, based on the notion that all actors in an interaction are simultaneously engaged in making such assessments and then acting on them.

All of this has been and continues to be the topic of much debate: What can be said about reasonable assessments by HE, given that HE is the stand-in for real-life individuals in our models? But, for current purposes, the important point is that when it comes to beliefs, mainstream economists are more than willing to get into HE's head, describing how she reasons and why.[1]

In comparison, when it comes to HE's tastes, the mainstream catchphrase is *de gustibus non est disputandum*, or "there is no arguing about tastes." HE comes with tastes, and mainstream economics takes those tastes as given and moves on.

The modeling restriction imposed on HE's tastes is that they *don't* change with changes in context. Consider the following story, which is depicted in figure 1.1: A man walks into a diner and asks for a cup of coffee and a piece of pie.

- "We have apple pie and peach pie today," he is told.
- "Yummy. Please bring me a slice of apple pie."
- "I just remembered, we have one slice of banana cream left, as well."
- "You also have banana cream? Well, in that case, please bring me a slice of peach pie."

This is viewed as irrational behavior without some untold story about how the existence of banana cream leads the man to infer that the diner makes a superior peach pie; for instance, prior beliefs that the existence of banana cream pie,

FIGURE 1.1 "Rational" diners don't do this. It's a violation of Arrow's coherence axiom.

while a priori unlikely, is correlated with superior peach pie. It leads to Arrow's well-known coherence axiom, which (in orthodox economics) describes rational choice:

> *If x and y are both available choices from both opportunity sets X and Y, and if x is among the best choices in X, and y is among the best choices in Y, then x should be among the best choices in Y (and vice versa).*

This axiom, imposed on an individual's choices, together with the technical axiom that something is chosen from every finite opportunity set, implies that the individual's choices can be rationalized by a complete and transitive preference relation. And, with a few more technical assumptions (say, existence of a countable order-dense subset), it justifies representing choice in that context as maximization of some utility function.

The one thing that is not a fit subject for economists is to try to say why, at the outset, HE prefers apple pie to peach pie. HE's choices reveal her preferences; they should be accepted, whatever they are. They are not something to be explained.

But what are legitimate arguments to place in HE's utility function? According to the *de gustibus* doctrine, anything is legitimate if HE's choice reveals her preferences along that dimension. This includes, for instance, HE's preference for a more equitable distribution of wealth in her country (or the world) or a preference to have the newest car on the block on which she lives. If this is what she prefers, *de gustibus* . . .

2

INTRINSIC MOTIVATION

This takes us to the category of *Homo economicus*'s (HE's) *intrinsic motivation*.

Fehr and Falk, in a survey article focusing on experimental work, provide three "categories" of intrinsic motivation: the desire to do things that benefit a specific other person (who generally does things for you); the desire to win social approval; and the desire to do tasks that are inherently fun or interesting.[1] We will take these in turn.

The desire to do things that benefit a specific other person can be modeled in two ways, only one of which (in my opinion) counts as intrinsic motivation. Suppose Jack sacrifices his own short-term interests to benefit Jill, because he expects Jill to reciprocate in the future *only if* he does this. This, which is typically modeled in a repeated-game setting,[2] is surely extrinsic motivation; Jack's actions are explained by the direct effect that his actions today will have on Jill's actions tomorrow. On the other hand, if Jack *internalizes* the welfare of Jill—if he would sacrifice his own short-term interests to benefit Jill, even if Jill's future behavior is unaffected by Jack's immediate sacrifice—then he is intrinsically motivated.

Similarly, Jack's desire to win social approval by (say) conforming to social norms, insofar as it is motivated by (a) a basic value he attaches to the social approval of others and (b) others providing social approval *only if* Jack conforms to social norms, should be coded as extrinsic motivation: Jack conforms to social norms to win the approval of others; the approval he craves comes from others. But suppose instead that Jack is wired to want to conform to social norms, whatever are those norms, as long as they are generally supported by his society, because his self-image is tied up in belonging to that society. This seems to me to be intrinsic motivation.

As for Jill doing things she finds inherently interesting or fun or, to add to this list, worthwhile; this is certainly intrinsic motivation at work.

The bottom line, at least in terms of my story, is that intrinsic motivation refers to "primitive" preferences of the individual. It excludes doing things because, by doing those things, others will respond in some desirable fashion. And insofar as we follow the standard economic tradition of revealed preference, this means putting in the individual's utility function arguments such as the welfare of specific others, the welfare of others generally, the desire to conform to social norms, and the desire to do tasks that are interesting, fun, and/or worthwhile. It is not something that is common in applications of standard microeconomics. But it is entirely within the standard paradigm.[3]

3

INTERNALIZING THE WELFARE OF SPECIFIC OTHERS

The idea that, in some circumstances, person A (hereafter Alice) cares about person B (Bob) and internalizes the impact of her choices on his welfare is surely uncontroversial. And it is easy to conceive of a model of this phenomenon. Alice's concerns for her own condition are encoded in a utility function u_A defined, say, on the social state $x \in X$ that her choices (and the choices of others) cause. Bob has a similar "personal-concerns" utility function u_B, defined on the space X of possible social states. And Alice, when contemplating which action to take (say, in some equilibrium of chosen actions, if the choices of others are involved), seeks to maximize some "greater" utility function

$$U_A(u_A(x), u_B(x)),$$

where $U_A(\cdot,\cdot)$ is increasing in both arguments. For purposes of tractability within a model, we might assume that U_A is additively separable:

$$U_A(u_A(x), u_B(x)) = u_A(x) + k_{AB}u_B(x),$$

where k_{AB} is a weighting variable that captures how much relative weight Alice puts on Bob's welfare relative to her own. (And there is no reason to restrict $k_{AB} > 0$ if we wish to model a situation in which Alice takes pleasure in Bob's discomfiture.)

As a sometime choice theorist, two things about this particular parameterization are of interest to me:

1. The notion of Alice's (and Bob's) "personal-concerns" utility function u_A is novel. In standard axiomatizations of preferences, no distinction is made between Alice's personal (or private) concerns and what might be called her "more general concerns," in which she is meant to care about how Bob feels about things. She has preferences that reflect her greater concerns; that's all there is.
2. And, in this parameterization, her greater concerns, insofar as they reflect her internalization of Bob's welfare, involve an increasing function of Bob's personal-concerns utility function.

To be a bit pedantic here, Alice's "greater" utility function U_A is an increasing function about how she feels about her own situation $u_A(x)$ and how Bob feels about his, $u_B(x)$. Compare this with an alternative formulation, in which we would suppose that U_A is an increasing function of u_A and U_B; that is, U_A takes the form

$$U_A(u_A(x), U_B(x)).$$

If we were to employ this formulation, and if Bob simultaneously internalized Alice's greater well-being with a utility function of the form $U_B(u_B(x), U_A(x))$, we must solve a fixed-point problem. It isn't necessarily a difficult fixed-point problem; with additive separability and $k_{AB} k_{BA} < 1$, we can resort to contraction-mapping arguments. But the formulation I'm suggesting is simpler, which begs the question: Is it a better representation of the idea that Alice cares about Bob's well-being and vice versa? I don't have a dispositive answer to this, but I can offer a few comments.

Suppose that Alice and Bob are the only two individuals concerned, and, moreover, social states x can be written as (z^A, z^B), where z^A is Alice's private consumption of goods and services and z^B is Bob's. In most economic models and, certainly, in standard general equilibrium theory, Alice's utility for a given social state $x = (z^A, z^B)$ depends solely on her own consumption z^A. By allowing Alice's personal-concerns utility function u_A to depend on both z^A and z^B, we allow, among other things, the following:

- Bob's consumption generates "tangible" externalities for Alice. If z^B includes Bob's consumption of a pleasant front garden, and if Alice and Bob are neighbors, Alice, holding her own "private" consumption z^A fixed, might prefer that Bob consumes more pleasant garden. If z^B includes some level of smoking tobacco, which generates secondhand smoke, Alice might prefer less of that for Bob.
- Bob's consumption generates emotional externalities for Alice. If z^A makes Alice well off and well fed, she may be unhappy personally if Bob is less well off or less well

fed. If Alice is a competitive sort, she may feel worse if z^{B} makes Bob better off than her z^{A}. (Concerns with income inequality and, on the other hand, "keeping up with the Bobses" presumably fit here.)

- Alice may have her own beliefs about what is good for Bob. Suppose Bob is Alice's young child. Bob may want a dinner of cake and ice cream, but Alice may prefer that he consume broccoli.

These are different from what I intend with $U_{A}(u_{A}(x), u_{B}(x))$. I intend that the three bullet-point phenomena just given are reflected in Alice's personal-concerns utility, $u_{A}(x)$. Her "greater"]utility function $U_{A}(u_{A}(x), u_{B}(x))$ captures, instead, both her personal concerns and her internalization of Bob's personal concerns. Mother Alice may prefer that her child Bob consume broccoli and spinach but, at least to some extent, she is concerned as well that Bob hates broccoli. She may regard kale as the best leafy green vegetable for Bob—that is, $u_{A}(x) > u_{A}(\hat{x})$ if x and $\hat{x}$ are identical social states except that $x = (z^{A}, z^{B})$ has Bob eating kale as part of z^{B}, while $\hat{x} = (z^{A}, \hat{z}^{B})$ involves $\hat{z}^{B} = z^{B}$ except that z^{B} involves kale substituted for chard. But she is overall willing for Bob to consume chard instead, if he hates kale and barely tolerates chard: $U_{A}(\hat{x}) > U_{A}(x)$ if $u_{B}(\hat{x})$ exceeds $u_{B}(x)$ by enough so that $u_{A}(\hat{x}) + k_{AB}u_{B}(\hat{x}) > u_{A}(x) + k_{AB}u_{B}(x)$.

To the three bullet-point effects listed above, I add a fourth suggested in Arrow's "Gifts and Exchanges."[1] The point of this exercise is to model Alice's internalization of Bob's welfare in her own general-concerns utility function. If Bob is better off, Alice is better off, and so Alice, insofar as her actions affect the true social state (the state x in which she, Bob, and everyone else shares), she takes how Bob feels about this into account.

Arrow (citing several prior writers) suggests that Alice may take particular personal pleasure from taking actions that help others in general. Insofar as this is true, such actions must, in this sort of model, be accounted for in u_A. But if these actions improve Bob's situation, they also impact u_B and so are "double counted" to some extent in U_A.

The assumption that Alice knows how Bob evaluates things—that she knows u_B—is unrealistically heroic. She might well internalize in her preferences Bob's welfare, honestly trying to appreciate Bob's perspective on things. But, in place of u_B in $U_A(u_A(x), u_B(x))$, we should probably have a real-valued function u_{AB} with domain X that encodes her perception of Bob's level of welfare or satisfaction or utility with the state of affairs. Mother Alice may not accurately appreciate the degree to which Bob hates kale, especially when we consider that kale-hating Bob, understanding that his mother wishes to take account of this distaste, will represent kale as much more unpleasant to him than is in fact the case. This raises several alluring issues that might be explored. For instance, in a long-term relationship in which the partners have these sorts of preferences, to what extent does each want to explain truthfully his or her personal-concerns preferences? In a dynamic setting, if Bob wishes to complain bitterly about kale, how much information can Alice gain about Bob's true preferences by observing choices he makes? (Alice says, "Fine, but if you won't eat kale because you dislike it so much, your slice of chocolate cake will be reduced.") How does Bob respond, knowing that Alice is making such inferences? In the setting of Alice the mother and Bob the child, perhaps such strategic considerations are too much. But what if Bob is Alice's employer?

WHAT IF BOB IS ALICE'S EMPLOYER?

This last question introduces the idea that employee Alice may, in work settings, internalize the "personal" concerns of her employer. Does the notion that Alice internalizes the interests of her friend or partner Bob extend to cases where "Bob" is the ABC Corporation? If Alice is part of a smaller team at work—think of Alice as a faculty member of a specific department—does Alice internalize the success of her department? In either case, is she willing to make personal sacrifices if it advances the interests of ABC Corporation or her department?

I contend that, at least in some circumstances, the answer is yes.[2] In support of this contention, I can offer somewhat indirect data.

For more than a decade, I taught in the Stanford Executive Program, which brings fairly senior executives to Stanford Graduate School of Business for a 6-week program in general management. Participants are roughly equally distributed in terms of domicile between Europe, East Asia, and America, the median age is late forties, the median organizational rank is senior VP/partner, and functional specialty and industry are both quite diverse. While teaching this audience, I survey them on what they consider to be "effective" motivation in their organizations, and one part of the survey asks them to rank the effectiveness of the following five motivational channels:

- tangible rewards (e.g., pay)
- intangible personal rewards (e.g., praise)
- interesting and exciting work
- work that contributes to success of the organization
- work that contributes to some greater social purpose

They are asked to rank each of the five channels in terms of its effectiveness in motivating themselves and, separately, their direct reports, and they are asked to choose the channel that "best represents" motivation for themselves and, separately, for their direct reports.

For themselves, "success of organization" is rated as the second most effective (close to interesting and exciting work), with 88 percent rating this channel as very or extremely effective. And a plurality (27.5 percent) say that it best represents their personal motivation. For their direct reports, it is also second (a more distant second to interesting and exciting work), with 75 percent saying it is either very or extremely effective, and it comes second in terms of "best represents."[3]

While these survey data certainly do not prove that employees internalize the success of their organization, they are consistent with this contention. And my casual empirical observation of the behavior of my faculty colleagues is that for some colleagues, sacrificing self-interest for the good of the organization is commonplace, while for others, it never, ever happens.

INTERNALIZATION OR ANTICIPATION OF FUTURE EXTERNALLY PROVIDED REWARDS?

One cross-tab in the surveys shows a significant difference between the ratings given by a subgroup of respondents and the rest of the respondents: individuals who identify as CEO, managing partner, or chair say that working for organizational success is a very powerful motivator for themselves. The obvious explanation is that for these individuals, their future fortunes are much more tightly bound to the fortunes of their organizations, both in terms of (likely) compensation packages and personal reputations, which may pay off in terms of future employment or simply prestige with and respect from others.

In general, any field "data"—including casual empiricism—that exhibit an individual seemingly internalizing the welfare of a specific other party can be explained at least in part as being motivated by the anticipation of future externally provided rewards. When Alice does a favor for Bob, perhaps she cares for Bob's well-being. But it is also possible that, as in formal models of trading favors, she does so expecting that Bob will reciprocate. An employee ranked lower than CEO may provide consummate effort on the job at personal cost in anticipation of being noticed by higher-ups, with a larger year-end bonus or a promotion in the offing.

To separate empirically internalization of the welfare of another from the anticipation of future reciprocal benefits, one must find examples of A doing personally costly "favors" for B in a setting where A's actions will never be observed by any party, either B or some third party, who can reward A for her actions in the future. This is a very tall order for empirical research; I leave it for those more clever in empirical design than am I (which, presumably, is just about everyone) to do so. Instead, I will assume that the basic phenomenon—party A makes choices that are personally costly to benefit specific party B because A cares about B's welfare—is real, and (near the end of the book) see where that assumption leads.

AXIOMATIZING THIS REPRESENTATION OF PREFERENCES

When I do this, I will employ the representation

$$U_A(x) = u_A(x) + k_{AB}u_B(x)$$

as representing A's overall preferences for social state x. How can we put this sort of parameterization on a sound axiomatic basis? How can we distinguish between what Alice thinks is good for Bob and her internalization of what Bob regards as good for Bob? At the cost of enlarging the space over which Alice's preferences are defined, this is straightforward to do.

The primitives are a set of social states X and two (or more) individuals, Alice and Bob, both of whom have "greater" complete and transitive preferences over social states. (To avoid technicalities, I'll assume X is finite; extensions to infinite sets of social states follow standard methods.)

Suppose we ask Alice to express her preferences over a larger space, $X^2 = X_A \times X_B$, where X_A and X_B are copies of X.

An element $(x_A, x_B) \in X_A \times X_B$ represents: Alice lives in a world where, for her, the state is x_A, while for Bob, the social state is x_B. Of course, this is an artificial construct; there will be one social state $x \in X$ for both Alice and Bob. But we imagine that Alice can contemplate a "richer" environment in which she lives in one social state and Bob lives in another. Moreover, we imagine that Alice can express preferences over such rich social superstates. We imagine that she has complete and transitive preferences $\succeq$ defined on the space $X_A \times X_B$ that, restricted to the diagonal in this space, are her preferences for feasible states, in which she and Bob necessarily live in the same world.

Embedding the "real world" in a richer choice environment to facilitate an axiomatic derivation of preferences over the real world is often employed in choice theory; e.g., in the classic paper by Anscombe and Aumann.[4] It comes with one philosophical disadvantage: In the currently canonical derivation of "revealed" preference, one starts with a choice function based on observed choice behavior, posits Arrow's coherence axiom plus some technical restrictions, and derives a preference-ordering representation with complete and transitive preferences. Adding in further technical assumptions, one gets a utility representation. But, by embedding the problem as one of preferences over a richer space, one cannot go back to observed choice behavior. Alice is never going to be observed making choices over $X_A \times X_B$. We must be comfortable thinking of her "expressing" preferences over this richer space or, alternatively, that we can impose restrictions on what her behavior would be if she could assign different social states for Bob and herself.

From here, the progression is obvious:

- Alice has complete and transitive preferences $\succeq$ over $X_A \times X_B$.
- Her preferences restricted to $X_A \times \{x_B\}$ for $x_B \in X_B$ are unchanged as you change x_B. That is, if (x_A, x_B) is preferred by Alice to (x'_A, x_B) for some x_B, then (x_A, x'_B) is preferred by her to (x'_A, x'_B) for all $x'_B \in X$. And, similarly, her preferences over $\{x_A\} \times X_B$ are unchanged as x_A is changed.
- Hence, we can represent her "personal-concerns" preferences—her preferences for (x_A, x_B) versus (x'_A, x_B) for fixed (and, by the previous step, irrelevant) x_B—with some "personal-concerns" utility function $u_A : X_A \to R$.
- We assume Alice's preference restricted to $\{x_A\} \times X_B$, which are independent of the choice of x_A, gives "Alice's-feelings-about-how-Bob-feels" utility function u_{AB}:$X_B \to R$. Immediately, Alice's overall preferences are given by some function $U_A(u_A(x), u_{AB}(x))$, where $U_A : R^2 \to R$ is strictly increasing in both arguments.
- Finally, assume all this is true for Bob's preferences, and that Alice's u_{AB} is "identical" to u_B.

Moreover, we can further invoke standard properties to get additive separability, using either Debreu's strong separability axiom or, what is significantly easier, using the mixture-space theorem, by placing preferences on objective-probability lotteries over social states, à la Anscombe and Aumann.[5]

EFFICIENCY?

If we agree to use this model, a question that arises immediately (at least, for economists) is, How should we define Pareto efficiency? Suppose there are three social states, x, y, and z, and two individuals, Alice and Bob. In state x, Alice has $48 to spend and Bob has $10; in state y, Alice has $40 and Bob has $20; and in state z, Alice has $35 and Bob has $30. In terms of personal concerns, both Alice and Bob are risk neutral over the amount of money they have to spend, and their personal-concerns utility functions are dollar denominated, so $u_A(x) = \$48$, and so forth.

Alice and Bob both have more general utility functions (U_A and U_B) conforming to the ideas presented here, but Bob is not concerned with Alice's welfare; that is, $k_{BA} = 0$, while Alice is very concerned about Bob, $k_{AB} = 0.9$. Hence:

$$U_B(x) = u_B(x) = 10, \text{ and so forth,}$$
$$\text{while } U_A(x) = 57, U_A(y) = 58, \text{ and } U_A(z) = 62.$$

I believe that any reasonable interpretation of efficiency would say that z Pareto dominates y, which Pareto dominates x. Efficiency, presumably, is based on the big-U values, not the personal-concerns little-u values. Certainly, if Alice had dictatorial powers to choose between these three states, she would choose z, and, just as certainly, if her choice is also the choice that Bob would make, that must be the sole efficient social state.

But would an outside observer, seeing only the physical outcomes (the amount of money each has to spend), see things in this manner? The point is that introducing the idea that Alice cares about Bob's personal concerns introduces a "positive externality," and, as is well known, this makes efficiency hard to observe from outside.

The notion of efficiency when one party or the other internalizes the welfare of another entity raises other issues if monetary transfers are feasible between the two. These will be met in chapter 12.

4

TWO (OR THREE) HETERODOX BOOKS

Some of the arguments entering *Homo economicus*'s (HE's) overall utility function that have been proposed here (so far) are atypical of economic models, but they are, at least at a theoretical level, within the realm of orthodox economics. If Alice cares about equity, Bob desires to do at least as well as his neighbors, and Carol has internalized Alice's welfare—that is to say, if their actions reveal that those are their preferences (with the proviso that revealed preference of Carol's alleged preferences presents problems)—who are we as economists to argue? *De gustibus* and all that.

However, if context or experiences affect their preferences—again, I should be careful to say: if context or experiences lead them to act in ways revealing that their preferences have changed—then we are breaking with orthodoxy. Two relatively recent books by distinguished economists do that. Another book straddles the fence.

AKERLOF AND KRANTON'S *IDENTITY ECONOMICS*

George Akerlof and Rachel Kranton's *Identity Economics* proposes that how individuals behave depends on their perceived identity, *which can change with changes in the context of their choices.*[1]

The idea that an individual's *self image* or *identity* affects their behavior is surely noncontroversial. Miller leads with the following story: When ready-mixed, boxed cake mixes were first put on the market (in the 1950s), they did not sell well.[2] It wasn't that the cakes—produced by adding water, mixing, and baking—failed a taste test. Instead, homemakers felt that use of the product did not conform with their self-image as homemakers who took pride in their baking skills. So, the manufacturers made the boxed mixes more complex: the user was required to beat eggs with oil and carefully fold the dry mix into the egg-and-oil emulsion. This made the mixes much more acceptable to homemakers of the time, and sales levels increased.

This is still within the realm of *de gustibus*. I doubt any economics paper has been written with such (revealed) preferences as are on exhibit in this story, but there is nothing here to contradict the standard paradigm.

What Akerlof and Kranton propose, however, goes further.[3] The individual agent has several identities: she is an executive, a homemaker and mother, a socially aware individual, and a market participant. And context triggers one of these identities, which then affects her behavior. To model this in terms of preference maximization, one must have her in-the-moment preferences affected by the context in which she finds herself, insofar as context influences her identity.

Consider, for instance, the use of stock options as a form of compensation in high-tech (and other) start-ups. One explanation for this form of compensation is that start-ups may be cash constrained. At least for some time (now no longer true), this form of compensation conferred tax advantages. Perhaps, although the tax advantages are gone, the practice became ingrained in the culture of high-tech start-ups; compensation in this form became an expectation that employers felt constrained to meet. And, insofar as the options only vest after a significant period of time, they may act as a retention device.

A story that makes less sense to an orthodox economist is that stock options provide economic incentives for employees: insofar as an employee's total compensation depends on how well the company does, this incentive story goes, the employee is motivated to work harder to make the company a success. Economic incentive theory teaches that incentives require a balance between efficient risk sharing and the ability of the individual worker to influence success. Where the individual has little control (the "outcome" on which the incentive compensation is based is a very noisy indicator of the employee's work choices) and the promised compensation is risky, such incentives are, the theory says, inefficient. Perhaps the balance of employee impact to compensation risk makes sense for a CEO, and even for C-suite level employees.[4] But employee compensation in the form of stock options is common at much lower levels in the organization, where the impact-to-risk ratio is tiny.

Identity economics provides a plausible motivational explanation: an employee who receives stock options thinks of herself as an owner of the organization and/or a member of the team that is working to make the company a financial success. This identity prompts an intrinsic sense of "responsibility" for the success of the organization, and, even if the impact-to-risk ratio makes no economic sense, the individual is motivated to do whatever she can to make "her" company successful.

Or consider the workplace phenomenon that exhibiting to employees that they are not trusted leads them to be less trustworthy. Initiating a regime of carefully inspecting employees at the end of the workday to keep them from pilfering company resources, it is alleged, will lead to more and more creative pilferage. If the "taste" for pilfering company resources were unchanging, any additional external pressure should, per orthodox economics, lead to less and not more pilferage.

David Packard provides anecdotal evidence, contrasting the tight control over tools and spare parts that he observed at General Electric in the 1930s with the policies he and Hewlett instituted at HP. He writes that at General Electric, "Many employees set out to prove this obvious display of distrust [was] justified, walking off with tools and parts whenever they could." In contrast, at HP, "open bins and storerooms were a symbol of trust, a trust that is central to the way HP does business."[5]

One possible explanation for this sort of behavior fits perfectly under the theory of psychological reactance, that individuals are motivated to regain freedom after it has been lost or threatened.[6] (See Steindl and colleagues for a summary of empirical evidence for the general phenomenon.[7]) In terms that Akerlof and Kranton might use, subjecting employees to stringent end-of-day inspections—a change in context—changes behavior in a way that is modeled as an increased desire to pilfer. If one accepts the theory of psychological reactance, it is not so much an increased desire to pilfer as it is a desire to gain (or regain) freedom. Observationally—that is, in terms of revealed-preference doctrine—it comes to the same thing.

An alternative explanation concerns the norm of reciprocity: the employee, offered trust, which he values, reciprocates with trustworthy behavior. Citing reciprocity may remind you of the discussion in chapter 2 concerning intrinsic versus extrinsic motivation: Alice, the boss, is certainly extrinsically motivated when she implements a policy of open bins and storerooms, in anticipation of Bob reciprocating with trustworthy behavior. But Bob's trustworthy behavior, in this instance, must be coded as largely intrinsically generated under the following circumstances: if Bob is one of many employees with access to the open bins and storerooms, his pilferage activities are unlikely to be detected by Alice as an act by Bob, specifically. Certainly, if many employees steal, Alice will notice that. And, in the face of such activity, Alice may well impose security restrictions. But Bob's decision to pilfer or not makes little difference to Alice's subsequent behavior. In an orthodox economics model, Bob reasons that whether or not he takes his share of the goodies, Alice's response will depend on the overall level of pilferage; Bob is largely a free rider. And, so, if he is inclined to steal, which he apparently is if tight controls are imposed, he presumably steals as much or more when there is free and unmonitored access to the goodies. But, per the *norm* of reciprocity, he does not. "Alice trusts me, and that changes my desire to steal from her." I think that this must be chalked up as intrinsic motivation.

So, which is it: reactance or a norm of reciprocity? In this regard, the reader is directed to an experiment by Burdin, Halliday, and Landini (commenting on Falk and Kosfield) that provides evidence in favor of reciprocity over reactance.[8] But whichever it is, it fits, I think, within identity economics. Tight control triggers an identity as an untrusted employee, which then gives satisfaction to getting away with theft. Open bins and and storerooms trigger an identity as a trusted employee or even "partner" who wishes to reciprocate trust with trustworthiness.

Stipulate that self-perceived identity can be important to behavior in economic situations. How should it be incorporated into formal economic models? Akerlof and Kranton suggest that an individual should be thought of as having two utility functions, a *consumption* utility function, the utility function that is standard in most of microeconomics, and an *identity* utility function, whose arguments (if I understand their proposal) are the level of adherence to the *norms* and *ideals* of the individual's self-perceived identity, and which (therefore) would be parameterized by that identity. That is, the identity utility function would look something like $v^I(x; i)$, where i is the individual's perceived identity, and x measures adherence to the ideals and norms of identity i. (The superscript I is for "identity"). The individual then "balances" her consumption utility and her identity utility by maximizing some increasing function of these two utility levels.

This two-utility-component construction is different from the two-utility-component function $U_A(u_A(x), u_B(x))$ of chapter 3. To employ the modeling suggestion of Akerlof and Kranton, while also providing for Alice's endogenizing the welfare of Bob, I suppose Alice's behavior would be modeled as maximizing something like

$$U_A\left(u_A\left[v_A^C(x), v_A^I(x; i_A(x))\right], u_B[\cdot]\right),$$

where u_A aggregates Alice's consumption utility v_A^C and her identity utility v_A^I, where the latter term is parameterized by her self-perceived identity $i_A(x)$ in social state x. I'm uncertain on what axiomatic basis one can legitimately separate consumption and identity utilities. Hence I prefer the simpler formulation in which Alice's "personal concerns" utility function is $u_A(x; i)$, her utility in state x if she perceives her identity as i.

The proposal, then, is that each individual's personal-concerns utility function is parameterized by that individual's self-perceived identity. And, the key step, perceived identity is a matter, at least in part, of the context in which the individual finds him or herself. The 100th employee at a start-up—say, part of the engineering team—perceives herself as part owner when she is compensated with stock options, versus perceiving herself as a "wage slave" when compensation is purely salaried. Because self-perception makes a difference in the maximizing choices made by the individual, the context in which choice is made influences the choices made.

Let me stress this point. If self-perceived identity is fixed and independent of the social context, reasoning about identity might help economists understand the choices made by an individual. This wouldn't do too much violence to *de gustibus*. It would be (only) a mild violation of the notion that economists shouldn't try to explain preferences. Greater violence is done to *de gustibus* if one grants that social context can shift self-perceived identity; this means Alice can manipulate (whether she is aware of this or not) Bob's preferences. To include this in economic analysis is, I think, wholesale denial of *de gustibus*.

Do individuals choose their identities? Can Alice manipulate *her own* preferences. I assume here that Alice cannot *consciously* do this. (But see Bénabou and Tirole for models where she can and does.[9]) However, before the book is done, I'll include the possibility—based on Bem's self-perception theory—that her choice of actions today, while not intended to change her preferences, can in fact do so.[10]

BOWLES'S *THE MORAL ECONOMY*

Samuel Bowles's *The Moral Economy* tackles the question: How and how far should policy makers go in designing extrinsic incentives—positive and negative—to promote "good social behavior" by citizens?[11]

While Bowles recognizes that self-interest powerfully motivates behavior, he believes that human beings are also naturally inclined toward cooperation and efforts to promote the social good. In *A Cooperative Species*, Bowles and

Herbert Gintis make the case that this is an entirely natural consequence of evolutionary processes.[12] Given this, and given his belief that "an erosion of the ethical and other social motivations essential to good government *could be* an unintended cultural consequence of policies that economists have favored, including more extensive and better defined private property rights, enhanced market competition, and the greater use of monetary incentives to guide individual behavior," then policy makers face some difficult trade-offs, unless and until they can find policies that support rather than erode the "good" social motivations.[13]

The key word in this paragraph is the highlighted "could be." This quote comes from page 2 of *The Moral Economy*, and a significant portion of the book is devoted to convincing the reader that "could be" should be "can be" and, very often, "is." Bowles provides a wealth of evidence in support of this, empirical and experimental, one example of which is the David Packard story I related in the previous subsection. And, once stipulated, he argues convincingly that policy makers who adhere too closely to orthodox economic thinking can do more harm than good.

I can't resist another anecdote from the IMSSS (Institute for Mathematical Studies in the Social Sciences) series of summer seminars at Stanford. In one session, the paper being presented was about income-tax evasion and "optimal" audit policies for the tax authorities to apply in view of such behavior. Hearing the topic, Frank Hahn (Cambridge University) sniffed and said (more or less verbatim) that, if a gentleman in England were caught cheating on his taxes, he would retire to his study and commit suicide in shame.

To which Bob Aumann (Hebrew University) responded that, if a gentleman in Israel were caught *not* cheating on his taxes, he would retire to *his* study and . . . I think you can guess what came next.

I suspect that Professor Aumann was just making a joke.[14] But, behind such a joke must be some element of truth. It is interesting to speculate on whether income-tax evasion was more prevalent in Israel than in England, and, if so, was there greater government scrutiny of tax returns in Israel than in England? And, if so, Bowles would ask, did greater evasion lead to greater scrutiny—the natural conclusion of orthodox economic thinking—or did causation also run in the other direction? Bowles's thesis, and one I endorse, is that greater scrutiny probably does induce greater cheating to some extent. The question is whether the economist's "direct" effect of greater scrutiny leading to less cheating exceeds the psychological impact of the lack of trust implicit in heightened scrutiny in terms of a greater license to cheat.

One of the empirical studies cited by Bowles is provided by Gneezy and Rustichini.[15] A day-care center in Haifa had the problem of parents arriving late to pick up their children at the end of the day. To motivate parents to be more timely, the day-care center imposed a fine for late pickups. Orthodox economics predicts that this will lessen late pickups; parents have whatever incentive they had before to be on time, added to which is a new financial incentive. Notwithstanding this implication of orthodox economics, the imposition of the fine worsened the problem of late pickups; parents were late more often.

Akerlof and Kranton as well as Bowles, each in their own way, offer an unorthodox explanation: in the no-fine regime, at least some parents (apparently) have intrinsic motivation to pick up their children on time. It is "the right thing to do"; a social norm, adherence to which is of fundamental value to them. In economic terms, their level of adherence to what they perceive as norms—or this specific norm—is an argument in their utility function, with greater "utility" associated with greater adherence.

But once a fine is imposed, the transaction, previously "governed" by a social norm, becomes a market transaction. The day-care center had established a price for being late, and the market trade-off of paying the fine versus personally inconvenient hurrying takes over. To use the language of Akerlof and Kranton, the parent of a child has an identity as a social actor and a different identity as a market actor. As a social actor, the parent feels and acts upon perceived obligations that come with good fulfillment of that role. But the imposition of the fine causes the parent to perceive his identity in this matter as a market actor, which releases him from social obligations.

In this regard, Bowles makes the important observation that the impact of the fine can be thought of as having two dimensions: *categorical* and *marginal*. The imposition of a fine of virtually any nonnegligible size has a categorical impact on parents; it shifts things from a social transaction with social obligations to a market transaction, for which different "rules" apply. The marginal impact of the fine, on the other hand, concerns the scale of the fine. If the fine is made large enough—say, the local equivalent of $100 for every minute the parent is late—one imagines that parents would show up on time. Indeed, given the uncertainty of traffic, one imagines that pickups would average several minutes in advance of the deadline (although such a draconian rule might lead many parents to seek different arrangements for their children, both because of the inconvenience of such a fine and because of the message this policy sends about the motivations of the caregivers at the day-care center). Bowles argues that a small fine—more generally, a small-scale financial inducement to behave—can be the worst of all possible schemes: it triggers the categorical effect, without being strong enough on the margin to induce the desired behavior.

BECKER'S *ACCOUNTING FOR TASTES*

Gary Becker's *Accounting for Tastes* (to some extent, reformulating and extending arguments from Stigler and Becker) explicitly tries to save "unchanging preferences" by modifying the arguments in the individual's utility function.[16] Quoting from the book:

> My approach incorporates experiences and social forces into preferences or tastes through two basic capital stocks. Personal capital, P, includes the relevant past consumption and other personal experiences that affect current and future utilities. Social capital, S, incorporates the influence of past actions by peers and others in an individual's social network and control system. . . . Utility at time t equals $u(x_t, y_t, z_t, P_t, S_t)$, where x, y and z are different goods. . . .

> [This] utility function itself is independent of time of the goods consumed and also of the capital stocks.

For instance, a reviewer of an early draft of the book suggests the following explanation for the empirical results reported by Gneezy and Rustichini: within the parent's utility function is the amount of "shame" the parent feels from his or her own actions. In the no-fine regime, being late causes increased self shame and decreased utility. But, if a fine is imposed, being late does not trigger shame. The idea in this explanation, and (insofar as I understand Becker) in Becker, is that the observed behavior—being on time or being late to pick up a child—interacts with *S* in different ways when a fine is imposed versus when it is not. This requires that the *S* variable include the social context, which may stretch what Becker intends, but if Becker can encode social context into *S* or *P*, his model is consistent with the observed behavior.

Or, in the story about pilferage and the explanation that depends on reactance, included in *P* is the individual employee's sense of autonomy. If constrained, Bob takes actions to restore his sense of autonomy. Or, in terms of the norm of reciprocity, Bob has an unwavering desire to reciprocate favors done for him, even if he sees no future benefit from doing so. (Bob, one might suppose, leaves particularly large tips when his experience at a restaurant is particularly positive.) Having been given the gift of trust, this aspect of his unwavering *S* motivates him to reciprocate with trustworthiness.

In these explanations, everything is "internal" to the individual. Consider, as an alternative, that a parent craves social approval from others; this is an argument of the (unchanging) utility function. In the no-fine regime, the parent believes that late arrival triggers social disapproval from others, be they the staff of the day-care center or other parents, especially from parents who endeavor always to be on time. But, once a fine is introduced, there is no social disapproval with being late; the day-care center has set a price, and the parent believes that others will conclude that "if the parent is willing to pay the price, it is no business of mine." This fits the Becker model, where there is an immediate (flow) variable for social approval, which interacts with Becker's social capital (stock) variable in a way that fits the story. But the social capital variable is somewhat unnecessary; this also can be construed to fit the "signal jamming" argument of Bénabou and Tirole, which I discuss in chapter 7.[17]

I'm of two minds about Becker's approach. On the one hand, unless there is some way to observe the values of P_t and S_t, and unless what we can observe—the choices the individual makes about the flow variables (Becker's x_t, y_t, and z_t)—are systematically related to the values of the stock variables, this is a difficult theory to test. On the other hand, while Becker is trying to preserve the notion that tastes, as expressed by his utility function, never change, he is definitely in the business of "arguing about tastes."[18]

5

CHOICE, PREFERENCE, AND UTILITY IN DYNAMIC CONTEXTS

In traditional microeconomics, dynamic choice consists of the static choice of an optimal strategy for current and subsequent choice, where optimality is based on initially given lifetime preferences, following which the optimal strategy is flawlessly implemented. If information may arrive through time that affects the individual's beliefs (using Bayesian inference), the possibility of adapting choice to what is learned enriches the individual's initial strategic options. But beliefs change only through the arrival of new information, which is incorporated into old beliefs via Bayes rule, and preferences don't change at all; at the outset, a well-considered strategic plan is formulated on the basis of those preferences and then carried out.

The justification for this heroic modeling convention is the typical economics shell game of beginning with a simple, reasonably intuitive example and then extrapolating wildly. Arrow's coherence axiom—the basis of revealed-preference theory—is introduced with something like the cartoon story of chapter 1, and then—often without any explicit statement—is assumed to apply to lifetime choices. If the context is an individual choosing what to order from a menu in a diner or even ordering groceries for the next week given the prices of the groceries and the individual's budget constraint, perhaps Arrow's coherence axiom—justified by the argument that the customer's behavior in the cartoon is unreasonable—is a relatively reasonable restriction to apply. But in the context of choosing one's education or career or on-the-job behavior for the next several years, this is, to put it mildly, something of a leap of faith.

A number of methodological arguments are given to justify this leap of faith:

- Anything else would be arbitrary, and with arbitrary modeling choices, the conclusions could not be trusted.
- Even if it is not how people behave precisely, it is a good approximation to real-life behavior.
- It may not be a good model, but it is the best we've got, and we can follow its implications and see where they lead.

There are, however, other systematic modeling choices one could make. In chapter 12, I propose models in which immediate choices conform to the standard Arrovian model of preference maximization, but choices made through time are not "dynamically consistent" in the usual meaning of that term. And to rebut the three excuses for the standard approach just given:

- Insofar as the linkages between successive immediate choices are systematic, models that are based on such linkages are not arbitrary. One can posit specific systematic linkages.
- I believe that, in the contexts I'll eventually discuss, this gives a significantly better approximation to real-life behavior.
- And, therefore, different assumptions—specific assumptions about how preferences at time $t' > t$ evolve from preferences, context, and experiences at time t—allow us to deduce implications and then judge, either with casual or formal empiricism, whether they do fit some real-life contexts.

One complication that I avoid in this book should be mentioned. Many immediate choices influence future opportunities. In formal theory, this is most simply modeled by supposing the immediate choice is of an opportunity set (or an immediate consumption bundle and an opportunity set) from which subsequent choice can be made. Two formal treatments of this situation that go in distinctly different directions are (1) the changing-tastes literature, begun (in economics) by Strotz, and (2) the preference-for-flexibility literature, for which I'll immodestly take some credit.[1] In the first case, decision makers, fearful of how their tastes will change, try to limit their later opportunities; the rubric "committing one's later self" comes to mind.[2] In the second literature, today's individual wishes to give one's later self some latitude to make choices the later self will consider best, hence the rubric "(otherwise undue) preference for flexibility." I avoid this complication here by avoiding choices that expand or limit later opportunities; but for a full treatment of the issues raised, such considerations are likely to be important.

6

SOME (SOCIAL) PSYCHOLOGY

Self-Perception and Attribution Theories[1]

Adding flesh to the bones of identity economics, psychologists tell us that an individual's self-perception at any moment is tied up with answers to three general questions:

- Who am I?
- Whom do I aspire to be?
- To what extent do I fall short of my aspirations?

The dimensions along which answers to the first (and second) questions are given include:

- personal traits, such as ambition, dependability, trustworthiness;
- skills and capabilities, from general skills such as the ability to analyze difficult models or to explain complex ideas clearly and concisely, to specific skills such as the ability to write excellent code in R or some other programming language;

- values, such as a belief in equality of opportunity together with merit-based rewards, versus a belief that equity demands equality of outcomes; and
- social identity (social groups to which the individual sees herself as a member).

Self-perception influences behavior because individuals try to act in accordance with how they perceive themselves. And, insofar as context affects an individual's (momentary) self-perception, context affects behavior. Hence:

- A parent, concerning his relationship with the staff of a day-care center, perceives himself as having obligations (values) of not abusing the staff by turning up late: he makes an effort not to be late. If, instead, he perceives himself as a customer who is free to "buy" whatever he wants if he pays the price, then once the day-care center initiates the fine for late pickups, he feels free to be late as long as he is willing to pay the price established by the day-care center staff.
- An employee at a high-tech start-up who perceives herself as nothing more than an employee has little reason to go "above and beyond" what the job nominally requires. But if she perceives herself as a member of the team, and if she values the success of her team, she happily goes above and beyond to do her bit in achieving success for the team.

While economists (generally) accept the doctrine of *de gustibus*, psychologists (perhaps I should say, some psychologists) believe that self-perception evolves, which then gives us dynamic choice that can and does reflect "changing tastes" or, more properly, changes in one's sense of self. This in turn leads to changes in behavior, which (insofar as "preferences" are the product of revealed preferences or choices) means changing preferences.

In *self-perception theory*, context and experience influence the evolution of one's perception of self.[2] Alice takes some action, somewhat without thinking consciously about the choice, and *after the fact* asks herself, "Why did I choose as I did?" The explanation—I would use the term rationalization, but psychologist colleagues wince when I do so—can be consistent with her self-perception, strengthening that perception. Or, in a given context, it can be somewhat at odds with Alice's perception of herself, leading to a reframing of that self-perception. Hence:

- The parent picking up a child at the day-care center makes a special effort to be on time. If there is no fine imposed for a late pickup, the parent frames this as evidence that he cares about the staff, which (in the future) strengthens the impulse to be on time. Or the parent frames this as evidence that he has a general social responsibility to adhere to "rules," which strengthens his subsequent adherence to this and other, similar rules of good social behavior. On the other hand, if there is a fine imposed, the parent can frame his behavior as the desire to avoid the fine, this time. His self-image with regard to this behavior is that he is making an economic trade-off. And so, in a later circumstance, he weighs the costs and benefits of arriving late as a matter of the financial cost versus the cost of inconvenience, making it more likely that he will choose to turn up late.

- A newly married individual, in the throes of romantic love, takes some action that is personally inconvenient but of benefit to her partner. She infers from this action that she cares deeply about the welfare of the other individual, which strengthens in the future the extent to which she does internalize her partner's welfare, leading to similar actions in the future. Or, if, following Becker's advice, she and her partner have a detailed contract that specifies what each must do for the other, she frames her action as "living up to the contract," which then guides her future behavior with regard to her partner.

Self-perception theory is a special case of *attribution theory*. In attribution theory (for instance), Alice observes Bob take some action and attempts to find an explanation for why Bob acted as he did.[3] The explanation can relate to the personal characteristics of Bob or it can relate to the external circumstances in which Bob made the choice. Insofar as there are several sufficient explanations that depend on external circumstances, Alice may build a "model" of Bob that links his behavior to one of those circumstances as it affects his personal characteristics. So, if Alice sees Bob hurrying to the day-care center to pick up his children, and if there is no financial penalty for being late, Alice may conclude that Bob values being on time. If she sees him behaving in this fashion when there is a financial penalty, she can attribute this to his desire to avoid the financial penalty.

This attribution of the other's motivation can and does spill over into one's own behavior, insofar as the "other" or "others" are members of a group to which (per her self-image) Alice belongs or aspires to belong. So-called social identity theory holds that individuals take on the beliefs, attitudes, and emotions that distinguish a valued group to which they (aspire to) belong and that distinguishes this group from out-groups to which they do not (and/or do not wish to) belong.[4] To give an example, suggested by my decade serving as senior associate dean of the Stanford Graduate School of Business (GSB), early-career faculty members usually seek to belong to the group consisting of their more senior colleagues. If those senior colleagues disparage the hard work involved in teaching MBA students (and, unhappily, some do), explaining directly or otherwise indicating that they do the minimum necessary to survive, early-career faculty members are prone to adopt this attitude, with the obvious consequences for their teaching. (This attitude is strengthened insofar as it distinguishes teaching at Stanford from teaching at the Harvard Business School.) If, on the other hand, an early-career faculty member observes her senior colleagues devoting themselves to teaching (at least, during quarters when teaching), and they attribute this to a combination of (a) teaching MBAs is not such an onerous burden, and/or (b) it is an important responsibility of being a faculty member at the GSB, then the early-career faculty member will adopt (a) the attitude and/or (b) the value, resulting in greater effort to provide a consummate effort in teaching.

And, to close the loop to attribution theory, the motivations of members of the in-group are not always apparent and must be discerned. Because context can affect attributions of the motivations of others, context in this manner can affect the attributes, attitudes, and values Alice attributes to Bob, which in turn influences Alice's behavior, insofar as Alice belongs or aspires to the group to which Bob belongs.

7

INTRINSIC MOTIVATION UNDERMINED BY EXTRINSIC REWARDS?

In the literatures of economics and of social psychology, a meme that is much discussed is that *extrinsic rewards can undermine intrinsic motivation*. Bowles provides a guide to some of the early literature.[1]

This meme was at the center of a public debate concerning blood donations in England circa 1970. Blood donations in England were (and, to the best of my knowledge, still are) done on a voluntary basis, managed by the National Health Service. A blood donor might be rewarded (tangibly) by a cup of tea and a biscuit, but that is all. Because shortages in available blood are general, a proposal was made to pay donors a fee, hoping that this added incentive would increase donations and relieve the shortages.

Richard Titmuss, a prominent sociology professor at the London School of Economics, argued forcefully that this would not only be ineffective; it would be counterproductive. In his book *The Gift Relationship*, Titmuss concludes:

> From our study of the private market in blood in the United States, we have concluded that the commercialization of blood

> and donor relationships represses the expression of altruism, erodes the sense of community, lowers scientific standards, limits both personal and professional freedoms, sanctions the making of profits in hospitals and clinical laboratories, legalizes hostility between doctor and patient, subjects critical areas of medicine to laws of the marketplace, places immense social costs on those least able to bear them—the poor, the sick, and the inept—increases the danger of unethical behavior in various sectors of medical science and practice, and results in situations in which proportionately more and more blood is supplied by the poor, the unskilled, the unemployed, . . . and other low-income groups, and categories of exploited human populations of high blood yielders.[2]

That is quite a list of adverse effects—and his list goes on beyond what I've quoted—and the meme can be read broadly as being about all of them: by taking an activity that involves citizens making selfless contributions (of no less than their blood) and turning it into a commercial transaction, adverse spillovers to all manner of social relations that rely on goodwill and trust for efficiency may be triggered. I don't mean to dismiss all these "unintended-consequence" adverse effects, if indeed they are there. Titmuss provides his evidence, which is based on (his) observations concerning the more "commercialized" blood-supply policies of the United States. (But see Arrow's essay "Gifts and Exchanges" for, shall I say, a more balanced analysis.) However, I wish to focus on the two most direct effects asserted by Titmuss. First (and rephrasing), paying for blood donations "represses the expression of altruism" in blood donations, lowering the amount of blood actually collected. And second (not part of the quotation, but one of Titmuss's other contentions), it will result in poorer-quality blood entering the overall supply.

Insofar as Titmuss's contention that "proportionately more and more blood [will be] supplied by the poor" is correct, he could both be right (in this contention) and be asserting that the policy is effective: *if* paying for blood donations increases donations from the poor (on the basis of their relative need for income) without decreasing (or increasing by a smaller percentage) donations from the more well-off parts of society, then, insofar as one accepts that the poor who give more blood are engaging in a market transaction that benefits both parties, the policy would be achieving its intended goal of increasing the supply of blood. But what the meme suggests is that at least some segments of the population will donate less blood if pay-for-blood is instituted.

If true, this is the day-care story once again. If all that is offered is tea and a biscuit, well-off Alice donates blood because she feels it is a social obligation, the right thing to do. Pay for blood, and what was a social obligation becomes a market transaction that she decides makes no sense for herself, because she is well off. And we can enlist self-perception theory: suppose a blood drive is run where Alice works. A group of her fellow employees goes as a group to donate blood to which Alice joins. But, after the fact, Alice tries to "explain" to herself why she did this. With no cash payment involved, she might see this as an expression of her altruistic nature. Or she might frame it as satisfying a desire to be a member in good standing of a group with which she identifies. But with a cash payment involved, she could believe that she—and her fellow employees—went for the cash. If self-perception leads her to believe that this is a worthy cause that her altruistic self should support, she might be more inclined to give blood outside of work. If her perception is that she did it because she is a member of the group, it might be neutral on her willingness to give blood outside of work. But if her perception is that she did it for the cash, then when it comes to private donations, which may involve more personal bother and expense, her "outside" giving in the future might well be chilled.

In the context of blood donations, Mellström and Johannesson provide empirical evidence from a field experiment.[3] Individuals were asked to give donate blood in one of three treatment groups. Group 1 was uncompensated. Members in group 2 were offered a token payment of around $7 to donate blood. Group 3 members were offered the same token payment but were given the choice between taking the money or donating it to charity. The authors report that among men, the different treatments made little difference. But women's behavior varied by group: women in group 2 were less willing to donate blood, although the ability to donate the money (group 3) fully counteracted the undermining effect.

Two papers by Bénabou and Tirole provide "orthodox-economics" rationales for behavior consistent with the meme, both of which are built on inferences rather than changes in preferences.

- In a first paper, Bénabou and Tirole suggest that Alice may be uncertain how painful will be the act of blood donation.[4]

"If," she reasons, "they are offering tea and a biscuit only, it probably isn't too painful." So, she goes to give blood. But if a monetary payment is offered, she assesses that it must be painful, reasoning that "to induce people to give blood, they must be paid." Wishing to avoid the prospect of pain, she demurs. The inference here is Alice's, of course.

- In a second paper, Bénabou and Tirole offer a "signal-jamming" explanation.[5] In the population, there are more altruistic and less altruistic individuals. Alice, at work, wishes for her peers to think that she is among the more altruistic based on a continuation function that gives her greater payoff in the future the more altruistic she is perceived to be. So, if all that is offered is tea and a biscuit, she can "signal" her altruism—even if she is not that altruistic—by going along to donate blood. However, if a monetary payment is attached, the signal provided by giving blood is less informative about the balance between Alice's altruistic nature and other concerns; balancing the two with such a "jammed" signal can result in a decision not to give blood.[6]

Both explanations work, in the sense that they provide equilibrium explanations for the undermining phenomenon, that the offer of a monetary reward might cause someone who would otherwise be willing to give blood to choose not to do so. (It is worth observing that Bénabou and Tirole's first model works when Alice is deciding whether to give blood in isolation; their second explanation requires an audience.) Whether they get at the heart of the undermining effect is another matter.

In particular, an early experiment that is cited as evidence in favor of the undermining effect involved nursery school children at the Bing Nursery School at Stanford University.[7] Without going too deeply into the details, students at the school were first given the opportunity to show intrinsic interest in the act of drawing and were classified according to how much intrinsic interest in this activity they exhibited. Then they were invited explicitly to draw for an adult in one of three conditions: group 1 was promised an "award certificate" with a gold star and red ribbon; groups 2 and 3 were not promised such a reward, but group 2 was given the "award certificate" at the end of the experiment anyway; children in group 3 did not get any certificate.

The experiments involved two outcome measures. The first outcome measure was whether, *subsequent to the experiment*, the child continued to show intrinsic interest in drawing. The data showed that children in group 1 had decreased intrinsic interest in doing so. The second outcome measure involved the quality of drawings prepared during the experiment; the data showed that children in group 1 prepared drawings judged to be poorer (by a judge who did not know the treatment-group assignments of the children).

One reason to mention this experiment is that it is doubtful that either explanation offered by Bénabou and Tirole can be said to be at work. The children, judged by their initial intrinsic interest in drawing, surely know how difficult the task is. And, so far as can be ascertained from the article, there are no peers around to be "signaled," even if one believes that nursery-school children are capable of the sophisticated logic of signal jamming. On the other hand, the external validity of a demonstrated effect on nursery-school children to, say, employees in the workplace or to blood donations is at best speculative.

Regardless of its external validity, this experiment is useful in that it allows us to propose three distinct hypotheses concerning how context—in this case, the offer of an extrinsic reward (and, for group 2, the granting of a reward without the promise)—affects behavior.

> *Hypothesis A. If the child is offered the opportunity to draw a picture by the experimenter, the promise of a gold star and a red ribbon leads the child to refuse the offer, relative to if no promised extrinsic reward is offered.*

This comes the closest to the blood donation story: the child only draws for the intrinsic satisfaction she gets; an extrinsic incentive on offer makes the activity unattractive. (This hypothesis also fits the Bénabou and Tirole's second story, but with a very different explanation.) I'm unclear on whether the experimental data were consistent with this hypothesis. Be that as it may, I am told by experts that the term *crowding out* applies to this effect.

> *Hypothesis B. If the child is offered the opportunity to draw a picture and accepts, the promise of a gold star and a red ribbon leads to lower-quality pictures relative to the situation where no extrinsic reward is promised.*

The paper reports experimental results consistent with this hypothesis. This mimics the day-care center story insofar as the fine reframes the "transaction." The child, for her own satisfaction, draws a beautiful picture. If she is drawing for the reward, her intrinsic motivation to draw a beautiful picture is diminished.[8]

> *Hypothesis C. Suppose the child is offered the opportunity to draw a picture and accepts. For children who are promised the gold star and red ribbon, their* ***subsequent*** *exhibited intrinsic motivation to draw on their own will diminish relative to children in the group who received no reward.*

That is, the extrinsic reward, even after it is removed, continues to affect the child's intrinsic motivation to draw. The experimental data are consistent with this hypothesis.[9] I am told that this hypothesis, if true, is an example of *overjustification.*

Hypotheses A and B are about in-the-moment behavior. They differ in terms of (a) the severity of the undermining effect and (b) whether commission of the task has a quality dimension. However, in terms of economic models, they are similar, in that they both concern changes in the in-the-moment intrinsic motivation (modeled via the preferences) of the individual. Hypothesis C, on the other hand, posits that context today can have lasting effects on one's identity; this is consistent with Bem's self-perception theory.

And, to finish the day-care story: the day-care facilities, seeing that the imposition of a monetary fine led to more late pickups, decided to cancel the fine. Unhappily, the incidence of late pickups did not revert to the original, pre-fine levels. At least in this case, temporary imposition of the fine had a lasting effect on parental behavior.

8

WHY ARE "SOCIAL PROMISES" UNSECURED?[1]

The constellation of ideas discussed in chapters 1 through 7 are, I contend, important for understanding how individuals behave in significant social and economic situations. However, while the discussion has been almost entirely verbal, the "standard" nowadays in microeconomics is that ideas are expressed, explored, and subjected to criticism in formal models. No economist was more responsible for setting this standard than Ken Arrow, which (to reiterate from the preface), in my opinion, was his greatest contribution to the discipline. Therefore, what comes next are some caricature formal models that illustrate these ideas.

The point is not only to express these ideas formally but also, with what I believe are reasonable parameter values, to show how powerful intrinsic motivation can be and how quickly extrinsic incentives, if they diminish intrinsic motivation, can become counterproductive.

I begin with a nearly trivial model. In this first model and subsequently, I invert the usual "the names have been changed to protect the innocent" to add some fun by using real-life names. However, the interactions in the model are (I won't say, entirely) fictitious.

Joe Stiglitz emails David Kreps and asks, "How would you like to come to Columbia next fall, to give the Arrow Lecture?" Kreps considers his workload and faces a difficult decision. He is a great admirer of Arrow, and it would give him great pleasure to give an Arrow Lecture. However, he is in the middle of a different and very time-consuming project that he is anxious to complete. He is unclear on which topic he might speak. And Stiglitz says that "a small book is customary"; Kreps knows how much work is involved in a book and is very hesitant. Notwithstanding all these concerns, after a bit of negotiation about what this entails, Kreps's admiration for Arrow wins out, and he promises to come. A date is set, the event is publicized, and, after arranging logistics, the day arrives, and Kreps either shows up or not. (Presumably, if he fails to show up, he gives Stiglitz something like a week's warning, offering some lame excuse that Stiglitz recognizes as a lame excuse.)

Kreps, in deciding whether to agree, faces the following problem. There are circumstances beyond his control that affect his ability to present the lecture. At the same time, his ability to show up depends on how much effort he puts into doing so. Let E denote his effort level, and let θ denote those uncertain circumstances; together, they determine whether he can arrive or not. Let $\pi(E)$ denote the probability that he is able to show up, if he chooses effort level E; suppose that $E \to \pi(E)$ is continuous, strictly increasing, strictly concave, and continuously differentiable. To begin, suppose E must be chosen before Kreps learns about θ, so $\pi(E)$ is the prior probability that he will be able to show up.[2]

Effort is costly to Kreps. Suppose effort E is scaled so that the (dollar) cost to Kreps of effort level E is E, which includes (for instance) the cost of spending time on this project instead of on other projects. Because he is a great admirer of Arrow (and despite his aversion to air travel), if he shows up and gives the talk, he gets a gross (intrinsic) benefit of B from doing so; this is gross of his cost of effort. Kreps is risk neutral; assuming he says yes to the invitation, his decision about E comes down to maximizing $\pi(E)B - E$. With the usual convexity/concavity assumptions, and assuming an interior solution, the effort level he would select if he agrees to the invitation is E^*, which satisfies

$$\pi'(E^*)B = 1 \quad \text{or} \quad \pi'(E^*) = \frac{1}{B}. \tag{8.1}$$

(Differentiability of all functions to the degree required is assumed at all times.) And his "participation constraint"—the condition required for him to agree in the first place—is

$$\pi(E^*)B - E^* \geq 0. \tag{8.2}$$

Stiglitz has a stake in this, as well. If he invites Kreps, Kreps agrees to come, and then Kreps fails to appear, Stiglitz is embarrassed. On the other hand, if Kreps appears, Stiglitz gets some benefit from the satisfaction of successfully arranging another Arrow Lecture. Stiglitz is also risk neutral, and his expected utility, depending on Kreps's choice of E, is

$$\pi(E)\alpha - (1 - \pi(E))\beta = \pi(E)(\alpha + \beta) - \beta,$$

where α measures Stiglitz's satisfaction if Kreps appears and β his embarrassment if Kreps fails to show, both measured in dollars. If we assume that Stiglitz's best alternative to Kreps gives him a net expected (dollar) utility of γ and that he (Stiglitz) can anticipate $\pi(E^*)$, the condition for Stiglitz inviting Kreps in the first place is

$$\pi(E^*)\alpha + (1 - \pi(E^*))\beta = \pi(E^*)(\alpha + \beta) - \beta \geq \gamma. \quad (8.3)$$

A PARAMETERIZATION

To carry along a fully parameterized version of this model, suppose $\pi(E) = 1 - e^{-\lambda E}$ for some parameter λ, so $\pi'(E) = \lambda e^{-\lambda E}$. The optimal E^* satisfies

$$\lambda e^{-\lambda E^*} = \frac{1}{B} \quad \text{or} \quad E^* = -\frac{1}{\lambda}\ln\left(\frac{1}{\lambda B}\right) = \frac{\ln(\lambda B)}{\lambda}. \quad (8.1')$$

This implies

$$\pi(E^*) = 1 - \frac{1}{\lambda B}.$$

Kreps's expected utility is

$$B\pi(E^*) - E^* = B\left(1 - \frac{1}{\lambda B}\right) - \frac{\ln(\lambda B)}{\lambda}$$
$$= B - \frac{1}{\lambda} - \frac{\ln(\lambda B)}{\lambda} = B - \frac{(1 + \ln(\lambda B))}{\lambda}.$$

This is nonnegative for all values of λB, but for this to make sense, it must be that $\pi(E^*) > 0$, which requires that $\lambda B \geq 1$.

Stiglitz's expected utility is

$$\pi(E^*)\alpha - (1 - \pi(E^*))\beta = \left(1 - \frac{1}{\lambda B}\right)(\alpha + \beta) - \beta,$$

So, for Stiglitz to extend the invitation to Kreps (rather than go to his best alternative speaker), we require that

$$\left(1 - \frac{1}{\lambda B}\right)(\alpha + \beta) \geq \beta + \gamma. \qquad (8.3')$$

BACK TO THE "GENERAL" MODEL

There are two immediate issues that arise. The first is that either inequality (8.2) or (8.3) may fail to hold. *In what follows, I will assume that they do hold; I'm more interested in Kreps's effort incentives.* The second (and, I think, more interesting) issue is that Kreps's choice of E^* does not take into account Stiglitz's interests in this transaction; Kreps's choice is selfishly inefficient from a social perspective.

Add an assumption that these utilities are measured where utils = dollars and that both parties' utilities are quasi-linear in monetary transfers between them. Then (based, for instance, on Arrow's compensation principle), the socially optimal level of effort for Kreps to choose is the level that maximizes the (unweighted) sum of the two parties' utilities,

$$\pi(E)B - E + \pi(E)(\alpha + \beta) - \beta,$$

for which the first-order condition is

$$\pi'(E)(B + \alpha + \beta) = 1.$$

Assuming no difficulties are raised with inequalities (8.2) and (8.3), this social optimum is easily attained per standard economic theory: Stiglitz offers an honorarium H if Kreps appears and, simultaneously, Kreps must pay a penalty P if he fails to show up. This makes Kreps's objective function

$$\pi(E)(B + H) - (1 - \pi(E))P - E,$$

hence, Kreps's first-order condition becomes

$$\pi'(E)(B + H + P) = 1,$$

and, as long as $\alpha + \beta = H + P$, Kreps will choose the socially efficient level of effort, denoted $E^{\#}$.

How do H and P affect the two "participation" constraints (8.2) and (8.3)? Begin with Stiglitz, *assuming that he must personally pay the honorarium and pockets the penalty.* Of course, Stiglitz probably doesn't finance the honorarium or pocket the penalty personally in the context of this sort of lecture. Columbia does, and we would need to understand the constraints Columbia imposes on Stiglitz in "making the deal" as well as the extent to which Stiglitz internalizes Columbia's financial position. But, for where I'm going with this, I proceed assuming that Stiglitz must put up the honorarium if Kreps appears and keeps the penalty if Kreps is a no-show.

Because $H + P = \alpha + \beta$, Stiglitz's expected utility is

$$\pi(E^{\#})(\alpha - H) - (1 - \pi(E^{\#}))(\beta - P) = P - \beta.$$

Indeed, if $H + P = \alpha + \beta$, and if Kreps appears, Stiglitz's payoff is $\alpha - H = P - \beta$, while if Kreps fails to appear, Stiglitz's payoff is also $P - \beta$. That is, in combinations of H and P that give the efficient outcome, Stiglitz faces no "dollar-denominated" outcome risk at all. (Therefore, at least insofar as we are looking for efficient outcomes, nothing changes if Stiglitz is risk averse, as long as Kreps is risk neutral. At the efficient outcome, Kreps bears all the risk. This, of course, will come as no surprise to readers who have studied agency theory.) And so, for Stiglitz personally to "finance" this arrangement, $P \geq \beta + \gamma$.

What about Kreps's participation constraint? His net expected utility is

$$\begin{aligned}&\pi(E^{\#})(B + H) - (1 - \pi(E^{\#}))P - E^{\#}\\&= \pi(E^{\#})(B + H + P) - P - E^{\#}.\end{aligned}$$

The following result is obvious.

Proposition 8.1. *Suppose that, with no honorarium or penalty, the choice of E^* by Kreps is such that both participation constraints (8.2) and (8.3) hold. Suppose that the honorarium H and the penalty P are set as follows: $P = \beta + \gamma$ and $H = \alpha - \gamma$. Then:*

a. *Kreps chooses the socially optimal $E^{\#}$.*
b. *Stiglitz is just willing to participate.*
c. *Kreps is also willing to participate.*

Proof. Note first that for this selection of H and P, $H + P = \alpha + \beta$. Therefore, Kreps chooses $E^\#$. And because $H + P = \alpha + \beta$ and $P = \beta + \gamma$, Stiglitz's participation constraint is met with equality. All that remains is to show that Kreps will participate, which is $\pi(E^\#)(B + H + P) - P - E^\# \geq 0$. Because (8.2) and (8.3) both hold, we can sum up the left-hand and right-hand sides, giving

$$\pi(E^*)B - E^* + \pi(E^*)(\alpha + \beta) - \beta \geq \gamma.$$

Substituting in $\alpha + \beta = \mathrm{H} + \mathrm{P}$ and $\beta + \gamma = P$, this is

$$\pi(E^*)B - E^* + \pi(E^*)(H + P) - P =$$
$$\pi(E^*)(B + H) + (1 - \pi(E^*))P - E^* \geq 0.$$

Hence, were Kreps to choose E^* when facing this honorarium and penalty, he would be willing to participate. Because he gets to optimize his choice of effort, he certainly will participate. ▪

The algebra may hide why this result is obvious. Setting $H + P = \alpha + \beta$ is socially optimal; this creates the biggest "pie" for Kreps and Stiglitz to share. Setting $P = \beta + \gamma$ gives Stiglitz a size γ slice of this pie. Because Kreps and Stiglitz would happily go along with a split of the smaller pie (in which Kreps chooses the inefficient E^* and Stiglitz takes γ or more), it must be that Kreps's slice of this bigger pie is bigger than what he got before; hence, his participation is guaranteed. (Of course, this all depends on the convenient assumption of transferable utility.) Indeed, although the algebra in the proof doesn't show this, it is clear that Kreps is not only willing to participate but also happier with this arrangement. If we set $P = \gamma + \beta$ and $H = \alpha - \gamma$, Kreps is getting the whole of a bigger pie less γ, while without any H and P, he was splitting a smaller pie with Stiglitz in which Stiglitz took at least γ.

STIGLITZ HAS ALL THE BARGAINING POWER

Because Stiglitz is doing the inviting, one might suppose that he sets the terms. If so, why would he set terms that leave himself with γ only? One imagines that Kreps and Stiglitz will bargain over the surplus created by H and P. However, in the spirit of agency theory, suppose that Stiglitz has all the bargaining power in this arrangement. He offers terms to Kreps, which Kreps must either accept or reject. We make the standard (and completely unrealistic) assumption that Stiglitz has full information about Kreps; in particular, he knows B and the π function, as well as Kreps's reservation utility level (which is zero).

In this case, Stiglitz could offer terms that make Kreps worse off than without H and P; if there is neither H nor P, Kreps's payoff is the left-hand side of his participation constraint (8.2), which we've assumed is nonnegative. Stiglitz, with H and P, and if he has all the bargaining power, can extract that value from Kreps (and more, by moving to the socially efficient $E^{\#}$).[3]

MAKING A DEAL WITH *H* AND *P* WHEN THERE IS NO DEAL WITHOUT

To keep the focus on the incentive effects of H and P, I (mostly) want to maintain the assumption that, without them, Kreps and Stiglitz can come to agreement; that is, constraints (8.2) and (8.3) hold at effort level $E^*, H = P = 0$. But it may be worth mentioning that, if either or even both of these participation constraints fail to hold when $H = P = 0$, having in place these two instruments, because they can increase the surplus to be shared, may make feasible an acceptable deal to both sides.

STIGLITZ HAS ALL THE BARGAINING POWER, BUT WON'T IMPOSE A PENALTY

What if Stiglitz has all the bargaining power but, for one reason or another—a reason why will be given shortly—he is unwilling to impose a penalty? This, we know already, rules out the possibility of a socially efficient level of effort by Kreps; to get Kreps to choose $E^\#$ and at the same time for Stiglitz to participate, we must have $P \geq \beta + \gamma$.

But an honorarium H might still be worthwhile. Write $U(H)$ for Stiglitz's expected payoff if he pays Kreps an honorarium H. What is $U'(H)$?

Kreps's first-order condition is $\pi'(E) = 1/(B + H)$, so an increase in H of size ϵ shifts Kreps's effort level by δ, where

$$\pi'(E+\delta) = \frac{1}{B+H+\epsilon},$$

(for E the effort level at honorarium level H). Assuming that π is twice-continuously differentiable, Taylor series expansions on both sides of this give

$$\pi'(E+\delta)=\pi'(E)+\delta\pi''(E)+o(\delta)$$
$$=\frac{1}{B+H}-\frac{1}{(B+H)^2}\epsilon+o(\epsilon),$$

hence, we get the relationship (up to first-order terms)

$$\delta\pi''(E)=-\frac{\epsilon}{(B+H)^2} \quad \text{or} \quad \delta=-\frac{\epsilon}{(B+H)^2\pi''(E)}.$$

Therefore, the increase in the probability that Kreps appears is

$$\pi'(E)\delta=\pi'(E)\left[-\frac{\epsilon}{(B+H)^2\pi''(E)}\right],$$

the impact on Stiglitz's expected payoff is

$$\pi'(E)\left[-\frac{\epsilon}{(B+H)^2\pi''(E)}\right][\alpha+\beta]-\pi(E)\epsilon,$$

and, therefore,

$$U'(H)=-\frac{(\alpha+\beta)\pi'(E(H))}{(B+H)^2\pi''(E(H))}-\pi(E(H)),$$

where I've now written $E(H)$ to indicate that E is the effort level that Kreps chooses at the honorarium H. At the value $H = 0$, this is

$$U'(H)\big|_{H=0} = \frac{(\alpha+\beta)}{B^2}\frac{\pi'(E^*)}{\pi''(E^*)} - \pi(E^*).$$

Proposition 8.2. *Suppose that, for all $H > 0$,*

$$-\frac{(\alpha+\beta)}{(B+H)^2}\frac{\pi'(E(H))}{\pi''(E(H))} < \pi(E(H)).$$

Then Stiglitz will never wish to offer Kreps a positive honorarium if he cannot complement this with a penalty for non-appearance.[4]

Because π'' appears in the denominator, this proposition isn't easy to parse. To make more sense of it, one can specialize to the specific parameterization $\pi(E) = 1 - e^{-\lambda E}$. Then π'/π'' is $-1/\lambda$, so

$$U'(H) = \frac{(\alpha+\beta)}{\lambda(B+H)^2} - \pi(E(H)).$$

This is declining as H increases, so it is clear that, in this specification, Stiglitz will not offer an honorarium on its own if

$$\frac{\alpha+\beta}{\lambda B^2} < \pi(E^*) = 1 - \frac{1}{\lambda B},$$

which is nonpositive if $\alpha + \beta < (\lambda B - 1)B$. If, on the other hand, $\alpha + \beta > (\lambda B - 1)B$, the optimal honorarium-on-its-own for him is the solution in H to $\alpha + \beta = (\lambda(B + H) - 1)(B + H)$.

A SECOND MODEL

As a variation on this basic model, suppose that the circumstances that might lead Kreps not to show are realized at some intermediate time, after Kreps has accepted Stiglitz's original invitation, and following which (but before the scheduled talk) Kreps can choose whether to overcome those circumstances. To model this, we bring θ, the state of the world, into the model. Suppose that θ is real valued and that Kreps, having observed θ, can choose whether to "overcome" the circumstances and appear for sure. Scale θ so that Kreps's cost of overcoming circumstance θ is θ and, on that scale, let F be the distribution function of θ (with support a subinterval of $[0, \infty]$). Assume that F is absolutely continuous, and let f be F's density function. Also, suppose that, prior to learning θ, Kreps incurs a sunk cost of preparation k.

In this formulation, Kreps's decision whether to overcome θ and appear (prior to the introduction of any honorarium or penalty for a no-show) is whether $B \geq \theta$; k, being sunk, does not affect this decision. Hence, once θ is realized, Kreps will appear if $\theta \leq B$, which is with probability $F(B)$, and his ex ante utility for agreeing initially is

$$\int_0^B (B-\theta) f(\theta) d\theta - k,$$

where we set his no-show, no-try utility (gross of k) to be 0. His participation constraint is that this ex ante utility must be nonnegative.

As for Stiglitz, in this formulation (and assuming Kreps agrees ex ante), he nets an expected $F(B)\alpha - (1 - F(B))\beta = F(B)(\alpha + \beta) - \beta$ if no change is made in Kreps's motivations.

But suppose that instead of $\theta = B$, the cutoff value of θ—the value at or below which Kreps appears, having overcome the adverse circumstances—is set at θ^0. Then the sum of Kreps's and Stiglitz's expected utilities is

$$\int_0^{\theta^0} (B-\theta) f(\theta) d\theta - k + F(\theta^0)(\alpha+\beta) - \beta$$
$$= F(\theta^0)(B+\alpha+\beta) - \int_0^{\theta^0} \theta f(\theta) d\theta - \beta - k.$$

The socially optimal level of θ^0 (assuming Kreps agrees and so the initial cost k is incurred), which I'll denote by $\theta^{\#}$, is the solution to

$$f(\theta^{\#})(B + \alpha + \beta) - \theta^{\#} f(\theta^{\#}) = 0,$$

or $\theta^{\#} = B + \alpha + \beta$. As in the previous model, if Stiglitz combines an honorarium H for appearance with a penalty for no-show, and if $\alpha + \beta = H + P$, Kreps will choose the socially efficient level of $\theta^{\#}$ as his cutoff. As in the first model, this provides Stiglitz with the payoff $P - \beta$ with probability 1; as in the first variation, Stiglitz's participation requires $P - \beta \geq \gamma$.

And, as in the first model, if Kreps is willing to give the lecture with $P = H = 0$, and Stiglitz is willing to have Kreps scheduled to appear on those terms, then setting $P + H = \alpha + \beta$ only enlarges the size of the "pie"; so acceptable deals between the two are still certainly possible. If Stiglitz is setting the terms as an economic-theory principal, he'll set the exact terms (the values of P and H) so that Kreps is just willing to accept. And, even if an acceptable deal is not possible with $P = H = 0$, including these terms, by enlarging the social "pie," may make a deal feasible.

This leaves the question: Suppose Kreps is willing to give the lecture, even without an honorarium. Suppose Stiglitz will not consider a penalty. Might Stiglitz offer him an honorarium, anyway, to raise the probability that Kreps appears? As in the first version of the model, we compute the derivative of Stiglitz's utility in H: if Kreps is offered H in addition to his intrinsic B, he chooses $\theta^0 = H + B$. Stiglitz's expected utility is

$$F(H + B)(\alpha + \beta - H) - \beta,$$

so the derivative of his expected utility in H is

$$f(H + B)(\alpha + \beta - H) - F(H + B).$$

The result parallel to Proposition 8.2 is much simpler in this case:

Proposition 8.2′. *Suppose that, for all H > 0,*

$$\alpha + \beta - H \leq \frac{F(H + B)}{F(H + B)}.$$

Then offering an honorarium can only be to induce participation. In particular, if f is nonincreasing, and if $\alpha + \beta \leq F(B)/f(B)$, this holds.

A PARAMETERIZATION FOR THE VARIATION

Suppose that $F(\theta) = 1 - e^{-\lambda\theta}$. Because

$$\begin{aligned} \int_0^{\theta^0} \theta F'(\theta) d\theta &= \int_0^{\theta^0} \theta\lambda e^{-\lambda\theta} d\theta \\ &= \frac{1}{\lambda}\left(1 - e^{-\lambda\theta^0}\right) - \theta^0 e^{-\lambda\theta^0}, \end{aligned} \tag{8.4}$$

we have the following formulas for this parameterization:

- Kreps's expected payoff (following some algebra):

$$B + H - \frac{1}{\lambda}\left(1 - e^{-\lambda(B+H+P)}\right) - k.$$

- Stiglitz's expected payoff:

$$(1 - e^{-\lambda(B+H+P)})(\alpha + \beta - H - P) - \beta + P.$$

WHAT IF A PENALTY DECREASES KREPS'S INTRINSIC MOTIVATION?

Notwithstanding the analysis just performed, I know of no real-world cases in which someone asked to give a named lecture is threatened with a penalty if she fails to appear. Honoraria are common, but my sense is that honoraria in such cases aim at getting the invited speaker to agree to come—that is, to satisfy the participation constraint—rather than as an after-agreement incentive device. (I'll discuss this further at the end of this chapter.) Perhaps the explanation is that invited speakers *always* appear or, at least, always make every effort to appear and need no further incentive. Perhaps a different form of incentive is involved; namely, the disgrace and loss of reputation that would result from nonappearance, which comes back to the absent speaker in the extrinsic-incentive form of fewer future invitations or simply social opprobrium. I don't doubt that such penalties do take place, however as I'll argue subsequently, without some modification in the story so far, this sort of penalty is an inefficient substitute for the simple imposition of a monetary penalty. And, yet, fully efficient monetary penalties are not, to my knowledge, ever employed.

This takes us, finally, to the point of these models (and the modification called for in the previous paragraph): What if, in the spirit of identity economics, the imposition of a penalty decreases Kreps's intrinsic motivation? With no penalty imposed, Kreps is making the journey to Columbia because he has long admired Arrow; it will give him a warm glow to deliver a talk in Arrow's memory and honor. With a substantial penalty imposed—and to reach the first-best while satisfying Stiglitz's participation constraint, the penalty must be at least $\gamma + \beta$—Kreps now considers that he must make the journey to avoid having to pay such a huge penalty. The warm glow, if not entirely dissipated, is at least somewhat diminished.[5]

The effect of an honorarium alone is less clear, and the language employed in calling the performance payment an "honorarium" and not a "speaker's fee" may well be at work here. On the one hand, with an honorarium in place, Kreps might begin to think that he is traveling across the country simply to earn the fee, with adverse implications for the warm glow. On the other hand, and especially if the honorarium is coming out of Stiglitz's personal pocket, it could trigger an intrinsic obligation to give a talk that Stiglitz in particular would appreciate. (This will come back in the next chapter, when we add to the model the effort Kreps must take to give a high-quality talk.)

So, getting back to the models of Kreps and Stiglitz, suppose that the imposition of a penalty $P > 0$ results in B decreasing to $\hat{B}$. Assume, for the sake of argument, that Stiglitz can offer an honorarium alone; if he does, Kreps's intrinisic motivation to appear remains B. Then Stiglitz's optimization problem bifurcates: he looks for the optimal scheme to offer Kreps under the constraint $P = 0$, but with Kreps's intrinsic motivation remaining at level B. And he looks for the optimal scheme to offer Kreps that involves $P > 0$, but with Kreps's intrinsic motivation being lowered to $\hat{B} < B$. Of course, in the second problem, we know that Stiglitz will necessarily choose H and P to satisfy $H + P = \alpha + \beta$ to get the "pie" that they share as large as possible; Stiglitz adjusts the levels of his utility versus Kreps's by changing the values of H and P while maintaining that their sum is $\alpha + \beta$ (where $H < 0$ is not precluded); and we know that the choice of P must be at least $\gamma + \beta$.[6]

Which of the two schemes—penalty or no penalty—is best for Stiglitz (and Kreps) depends on all the parameters of the model. Parameter values can be arranged so that Stiglitz lives with the $H = P = 0$ arrangement, or with $P = 0$ and some $H > 0$, or with $H + P = \alpha + \beta$. One can prove obvious "comparative statics" results, for instance: *All other parameters held fixed, if Stiglitz chooses "leave well enough alone," in the sense that he chooses $P = 0$ for a set of parameter values including $\hat{B}$, then he will do the same for the same parameters except that $\hat{B}$ changes to $\check{B} < \hat{B}$.* And so forth. Rather than chase down all such results, I'll illustrate with the specific parameterization for the second-variation model, together with some "reasonable" parameter values. (The first-variation model, with "identity economics" effects, will reappear in chapter 9, when the story is enriched with multitasking.)

Begin with the initial position, in which Kreps chooses $\theta = B$. Kreps does in fact have a lot of intrinsic motivation to deliver this lecture, and so I choose $B = \$20{,}000$. (Would I pay $20,000 out of pocket for the privilege of giving the Arrow Lecture? My admiration for Arrow is very great, and this is not an absurd number.) It is somewhat costly for him to prepare the talk; set $k = \$10{,}000$. I choose λ so that Kreps, on his own, is very likely to choose to appear; I make the probability of appearance (no honorarium or penalty) 0.95, so $F(20{,}000) = 1 - e^{-\lambda 20{,}000} = 0.95$, which gives $\lambda = -\ln(0.05)/20{,}000 = 0.00015$, to the fifth digit. This gives Kreps the expected payoff of

$$B - \frac{1}{\lambda}\left(1 - e^{-\lambda B}\right) - k = \$20{,}000 - 0.95/0.000015 - \$10{,}000$$
$$= \$3{,}657.64$$

So, Kreps is happy to appear.

Stiglitz's three parameters are α, β, and γ. Taking γ first, I'll assume that Stiglitz's best alternative to Kreps provides him with a net \$7,000 of utility. He prefers Kreps to this alternative if Kreps will appear: α = \$10,000. But it is very embarrassing to him if Kreps fails to show: β = \$20,000. Hence, with $H = P = 0$, Stiglitz's expected utility of dealing with Kreps is

$$0.95 \times \$10{,}000 - 0.05 \times \$20{,}000 = \$8{,}500;$$

Kreps is better than Stiglitz's next best alternative, if Stiglitz chooses $H = P = 0$.

Now, just to check, suppose that imposing a penalty and honorarium doesn't change Kreps's intrinsic motivation B. Stiglitz chooses the socially efficient values $H + P$ = \$30,000, and Kreps chooses $\theta^{\#}$—the cutoff effort level for appearing—to be $B + H + P$ = \$50,000. This gives a probability of $1 - e^{-0.000015 \times 50{,}000} = 0.99944$. To determine the payoffs of the two parties, we must fix how H and P are set so that $H + P = \alpha + \beta$. First, suppose we set $P = \beta + \gamma$ = \$27,000, so Kreps's honorarium is \$3,000. This gives Stiglitz a for-certain payoff of \$7,000 (of course), and it gives Kreps an expected payoff of \$6,327.57. Note that the sum of their expected payoffs is \$13,327.57 versus a sum-of-payoffs of \$12,157 if $H = P = 0$.

To get Stiglitz to his original expected payoff of \$8,500, we must set H = \$1,500 and P = \$28,500. This gives Stiglitz a for-sure payoff of \$8,500 and lowers Kreps's expected payoff to \$4,827.57, better than with $H = P = 0$. (Of course, the sum of these expected payoffs is the same \$13,327.57.)

Stiglitz might look for terms that reduce Kreps's expected payoff to his participation level payoff of zero. But, with these numbers, this presents a problem: if Stiglitz chooses $P + H = \alpha + \beta = \$30{,}000$ and makes it all penalty—that is, $H = 0$ and $P = \$30{,}000$, Kreps's expected payoff is still positive, equal to $3,327.59. (Stiglitz's payoff is $10,000.) To reduce Kreps's expected payoff further (with these numbers), while maintaining efficiency, Stiglitz must make $H < 0$. That is, he proposes to Kreps that, if Kreps comes and gives the lecture, he (Kreps) will need to give Stiglitz a small fee for the opportunity. And if Kreps fails to show, he must pay a big penalty. The numbers that get Kreps's expected payoff to zero are $H = -\$3{,}327.59$ and $P = \$33{,}327.59$; of course, Stiglitz now captures all the social surplus.

I've assumed that if Stiglitz sets $P = 0$ but $H > 0$, he does not reduce Kreps's intrinsic motivation. So, would he wish to do so? *If* Stiglitz would only set $H > 0$ if it increased his expected payoff from the base level of $8,500, the answer is no; any $H > 0$ reduces Stiglitz's payoff. On the other hand, if he is willing to settle for less expected payoff—if, for instance, he is willing to set $H > 0$ to increase social welfare, as long as he is left with his reservation payoff of $7,000—then an honorarium of $1,953.40 (and $P = 0$) leaves him with an expected payoff of $7,000 and increases Kreps's payoff to $5,525.98, while increasing the probability that Kreps appears to 0.9627.

Now we come to the point of this exercise: if Stiglitz's proposal includes a penalty of any size, this will diminish Kreps's intrinsic motivation to appear, *B*. And, *B* is reduced a discrete amount by any size penalty; in the terminology of Bowles, the impact of a penalty on *B* is categorical, not marginal.[7] To reiterate, this is the Israeli day-care center/identity economics again: if a penalty is imposed, Kreps reframes his efforts to appear as avoiding the penalty. He may still get some intrinsic reward for showing up, but less than before.

How much less? Begin with supposing that $\hat{B}$ is half of B, or \$10,000. Suppose Stiglitz imposes the minimum penalty consistent with keeping his (Stiglitz's) payoff at or above his reservation level of \$7,000; that, of course, is $P = \gamma + \beta =$ \$27,000, hence, $H =$ \$3,000. With the added incentive to appear, the probability that Kreps shows up does indeed rise, to 0.9975.[8] However, Kreps's expected payoff is −\$3,659.47; Kreps will not agree a priori. *If the imposition of a penalty—and the penalty must be at least \$27,000 for Stiglitz to be satisfied—causes Kreps's intrinsic incentive to halve, no acceptable deal between Kreps and Stiglitz is possible with a penalty.*

If you think that halving Kreps's intrinsic motivation is severe, questions worth answering are: How far can B fall and still have a possible deal between the two? How far can B fall and leave the sum of the two payoffs at least as large as with $H = P = 0$?

- For an acceptable deal—Stiglitz's expected payoff is at least \$7,000 and Kreps's is at least \$0—Kreps's after-penalty intrinsic motivation B must be at least \$13,666.53. This is achieved with $P =$ \$27,000 and $H =$ \$3,000, of course, making the probability of Kreps appearing equal to 0.99856. Equally of course, this gives a sum of payoffs of \$7,000, a good deal less than the sum of payoffs with no penalty, which is \$12,157.64.
- So that the sum of payoffs is at least \$12,157.64— that is, an honorarium and penalty give a more socially efficient

outcome than the $H = P = 0$ outcome—Kreps's after-penalty instrinsic motivation must exceed (approximately) \$18,829.36. *For this parameterization, if the imposition of a penalty leads Kreps's intrinsic motivation to decrease by \$1,171 or more from a starting level of \$20,000, Stiglitz and Kreps are jointly better off with $H = P = 0$.*

- One should not conclude that if, say, imposing a penalty will cause Kreps's intrinsic motivation term to fall to \$17,000 (enough so that the sum of expected payoffs is less than in the base case), then Stiglitz will choose not to impose a penalty. If, for instance, Stiglitz imposes $P =$ \$30,000 (and, to be socially efficient, $H = 0$) and if this causes Kreps's intrinsic motivation to decrease to \$17,000, Stiglitz's expected payoff will be \$10,000, while Kreps nets an expected \$329.69. That is, from Stiglitz's selfish perspective, starting from the base case, if he wishes to "transfer" payoff to himself from Kreps, whose expected payoff in the base case is \$3,657.64, imposing a penalty will work (as long as Kreps's new $\hat{B}$ isn't too small). It isn't a dollar-for-dollar transfer; to affect a transfer, Stiglitz must make $P > 0$, which destroys social surplus. But, at least for $\hat{B} =$ \$17,000, a penalty of \$30,000 will make Stiglitz \$1,500 better off in expected payoff, at a cost of reducing Kreps's expected payoff by more than \$3,300.

All these numbers are summarized in tables 8.1 and 8.2.

This is a very simple model, and it may be that the math is hiding what is going on. As agency problems go, this one is extremely simple. Both parties are risk neutral, and they can transfer payoff = money between one another. So, once it is

Table 8.1 Some Numbers for the Base Model

	Scenario A	Scenario B	Scenario C	Scenario D	Scenario E
B	\$20,000.00	\$20,000.00	\$20,000.00	\$20,000.00	\$20,000.00
H	\$0	\$1,953.00	\$3,000.00	\$1,500.00	−\$3,327.57
P	\$0.00	\$0.00	\$27,000.00	\$28,500.00	\$33,327.57
Probability Kreps appears	0.9500	0.9627	0.99944	0.99944	0.99944
Kreps's payoff	\$3,657.64	\$5,525.98	\$6,327.57	\$4,827.57	\$0.00
Stiglitz's payoff	\$8,500.00	\$7,000.33	\$7,000.00	\$8,500.00	\$13,327.57
sum of payoffs	\$12,157.64	\$12,526.31	\$13,327.57	\$13,327.57	\$13,327.57

Note: This table provides numbers for five scenarios. The following parameters are fixed: $\lambda = 0.00015$, $k = \$10,000$, $\alpha = \$10,000$, $\beta = \$20,000$, and $\lambda = \$7,000$. Scenario A gives the outcome for $H = P = 0$, the benchmark in which Stiglitz invites Kreps with no money involved. Scenario B has $H = \$1,953$ and $P = 0$. Because $P = 0$, Kreps's intrinsic motivation to appear, B, remains \$20,000; this honorarium is the most Stiglitz can offer while meeting his participation constraint. Note that this increases social welfare. Scenarios C, D, and E assume that the imposition of a penalty does not decrease B; in scenario C, Stiglitz settles for his reservation payoff; in scenario D, he insists that he himself is no worse off than scenario A. In scenario E, Stiglitz proposes terms that pull Kreps down to his reservation payoff level.

decided to move away from the base case of $H = P = 0$ and, in particular, to impose a strictly positive penalty, from the perspective of the sum of the two parties' expected payoffs, they will move to the socially efficient arrangement, which is $H + P = \alpha + \beta = \$30,000$. How the social "surplus" is split between them is determined by how the \$30,000 is split between H and P; more H is good for Kreps; more P is good for Stiglitz.

In terms of the "social surplus" created by any deal—that is to say, *ignoring transfers*—there are three factors to consider:

1. Because $P + H > 0$ increases Kreps's probability of appearance, Stiglitz gets $\alpha = \$10,000$ with higher probability and loses $\beta = \$20,000$ with lower probability.

Table 8.2 More Numbers for the Base Model

	Scenario A	Scenario F	Scenario G	Scenario H	Scenario J
$\hat{B}$	\$20,000.00	\$10,000.00	\$13,666.53	\$18,829.36	\$17,000.00
H	\$0.00	\$3,000.00	\$3,000.00	\$3,000.00	\$0.00
P	\$0.00	\$27,000.00	\$27,000.00	\$27,000.00	\$30,000.00
Probability Kreps appears	0.9500	0.99750	0.99856	0.99933	0.99912
Kreps's payoff	\$3,657.64	–\$3,659.47	\$0.00	\$5,157.64	\$329.69
Stiglitz's payoff	\$8,500.00	\$7,000.00	\$7,000.00	\$7,000.00	\$10,000.00
Sum of payoffs	\$12,157.64	\$3,340.53	\$7,000.00	\$12,157.64	\$10,329.69

Note: This table compares the base scenario A with scenarios in which the imposition of a positive penalty causes Kreps's implicit motivation to decrease. In scenario F, it is assumed that imposing a penalty causes B to halve, to \$10,000; the sum of payoffs (at the efficient combination of H and P) is such that no deal is feasible. Scenario G records that, if Kreps's intrinsic motivation falls to \$13,666.53, a deal is just feasible. Note, however, that this is less efficient than when $P = 0$. Scenario H indicates that if Kreps's intrinsic motivation falls to \$18,829.36 (only), then an efficient H and P leave the "pie" to be shared by Kreps and Stiglitz the same size as when $H = P = 0$. Scenario J illustrates that, even if a penalty reduces Kreps's intrinsic motivation enough so that social welfare is reduced, Stiglitz might still impose a penalty to increase his own expected payoff.

2. But Kreps incurs additional real costs, in the amount

$$\int_{\theta=B}^{\theta=\hat{B}+H+P} \theta\lambda e^{-\lambda\theta}\, d\theta.$$

(Even if $\hat{B} = 0$, $H + P = \$30{,}000$ implies that $\hat{B} + H + P > B$.)

3. And even though the probability that Kreps appears increases, which means that he gets to "enjoy" $\hat{B}$ more often, it is the product of the probability that he appears times $\hat{B}$ that matters. That is, the new and higher probability of appearance times the new $\hat{B}$ may be less than $0.95 \times \$20{,}000$, the original values.

Table 8.3 "Real" Effects of $P > 0$ in the Scenarios of Table 8.2

	Scenario A	Scenario F	Scenario G	Scenario H	Scenario J
$\hat{B}$	\$20,000.00	\$10,000.00	\$13,666.53	\$18,829.36	\$17,000.00
H	\$0.00	\$3,000.00	\$3,000.00	\$3,000.00	\$0.00
P	\$0.00	\$27,000.00	\$27,000.00	\$27,000.00	\$30,000.00
Probability Kreps appears	0.95	0.99750	0.99856	0.99933	0.99912
Change for Stiglitz	\$0.00	\$1,425.00	\$1,456.69	\$1,480.02	\$1,473.72
Additional cost for Kreps	\$0.00	\$1,217.12	\$1,261.14	\$1,296.83	\$1,286.78
Net change in Kreps's expected enjoyment	\$0.00	–\$9,025.00	–\$5,353.20	–\$183.18	–\$2,014.89
Net change in the size of the pie from base case	\$0.00	–\$8,817.12	–\$5,157.64	\$0.00	–\$1,827.96

These "real" changes for the scenarios in table 8.2 are provided in table 8.3. Note in particular that in the three scenarios where Kreps's intrinsic motivation decreases from \$20,000, the third real change—his new, lower $\hat{B}$ times the new, higher probability of appearing—is, on net, less than \$20,000 × 0.95. This does not happen if the new $\hat{B}$ term is close to \$20,000. And, of course, in all cases, the additional cost for him exceeds any possible real benefits he receives.

KREPS'S INITIAL INTRINSIC MOTIVATION ISN'T SO LARGE

Go back to table 8.1 and the observation that, in the base case of $H = P = 0$, social surplus is \$12,157.64, while the first-best social surplus—with $H + P = \$30{,}000$ and assuming that Kreps's intrinsic motivation does not decrease with the imposition of a penalty—is \$13,327.57. That isn't a huge gain, and it explains to some extent why, in this model with the numbers I've used, Stiglitz may well decide against chasing the "efficient" arrangement if it means a substantial reduction in Kreps's intrinsic motivation. Kreps comes with plenty of intrinsic motivation—he appears with probability 0.95 if Stiglitz leaves well enough alone—and there is little that Stiglitz can accomplish by adding in further extrinsic incentives.

But suppose instead that we begin with $B = \$10{,}000$ and $k = \$5{,}000$. Kreps has lower costs but also lower initial intrinsic motivation.

- At $H = P = 0$, Kreps only appears with probability 0.7764, his expected utility is −\$183.33, and Stiglitz's expected payoff is \$3,291.80 (so, neither participation constraint is met). Social surplus is only \$3,108.47.
- If imposing a penalty does not reduce Kreps's intrinsic motivation from its initial level of \$10,000, and if Stiglitz chooses the first-best $H + P = \$30{,}000$, Kreps appears with probability 0.9975, and social surplus jumps to \$8,340.53. So, choosing P between \$27,000 and \$28,340.53 will meet Kreps's participation constraint and provide Stiglitz with a for-certain payoff between \$7,000 and \$8,340.53.
- If imposing a penalty would decrease Kreps's intrinsic motivation from its initial level of \$10,000 and if, in consequence, Stiglitz decides not to impose a penalty but to try instead $H > 0$, an acceptable deal between the two is impossible: It takes an honorarium of at least \$235 to get

Kreps to appear, at which point Stiglitz's expected payoff is only \$3,339.54. But, in this case, a still higher honorarium improves both payoffs. The optimal honorarium for Stiglitz to set, to maximize his own expected payoff, is H = \$1,150.02: Kreps's expected payoff rises to \$737.77, and Stiglitz's expected payoff is \$3,419.74. But this is still not enough to meet Stiglitz's participation constraint.

- And, if imposing a penalty reduces Kreps's intrinsic motivation below its initial level of \$10,000: The cutoff level of $\hat{B}$ (Kreps's new intrinsic motivation), below which no deal is possible, is \$8,656. At this level of intrinsic motivation for Kreps, and with H = \$3,000 and P = \$27,000, Stiglitz's payoff is \$7,000, and Kreps's expected payoff is \$0.25. (Kreps shows up with probability 0.9969.)

The obvious conclusion is . . . obvious. When Kreps has a lot of intrinsic motivation, enough so that an acceptable deal is possible, and if imposing a penalty decreases that intrinsic motivation, Stiglitz is often best off by leaving well enough alone. But when Kreps has less intrinsic motivation, and even if imposing a penalty will decrease that intrinsic motivation, Stiglitz may have no choice but to go with some extrinsic incentives to make a deal possible.

DOES THIS EXPLAIN WHY WE DON'T SEE PENALTY CLAUSES IN REAL-WORLD SOCIAL EXCHANGE?

The issue here is broader than invited lectures. Consider the variety of "social favors" that one party, Alice, asks Bob to perform. These can be as prosaic as driving Alice to the airport or taking her home from the airport, to helping her move to a new apartment, to helping her prepare for an exam that she must take. Alice asks Bob, "Will you?," and if Bob responds that he will, Alice expects that he will come through. However, "coming through" requires Bob to put in some level of costly effort, and circumstances may arise that lead Bob to renege on his promise to perform.

Bob's motivation to perform can come from (at least) three sources. First, he may get satisfaction from the act of doing this sort of favor for anyone. That is, he enjoys doing favors. He may internalize Alice's welfare and gain satisfaction from doing a favor for her, specifically. (Does Kreps internalize Stiglitz's welfare? I'll leave that for your own speculation.) And—the typical explanation in economics—he may anticipate that Alice or friends of Alice will later have the opportunity to reciprocate and do favors for him, but only if he does this favor for her. Of course, the first two fit into the category of intrinsic motivation, while the third is based on extrinsic incentives.

All of these motivations can be incorporated within "standard economics," although only the last is typical in the literature; allowing Bob to get satisfaction from doing favors in general or from his internalization of Alice's welfare is . . . uncommon. And, if what motivates Bob is strong enough so that he never fails to do the favor, the story ends there. But what if, in some circumstances, the personal cost to Bob of doing the favor is such that he defaults? What if, in some circumstances, the personal cost to him exceeds the benefit to Alice, so it is efficient not to do some favors. Think here of situations in which the costs to Bob and benefits to Alice are realized only after Alice asks Bob for the favor. On the basis of an ex ante calculation, Bob may agree to provide the requested favor, but, when it comes time to perform, the realized cost to him may be much more than he anticipated on average. And, to complicate this story further, think of a case in which only Bob sees the cost to him; if he fails to carry out the favor, he offers an excuse to Alice, but she cannot verify the excuse's bona fides.

If there are no consequences for Bob for failing to carry out the favor, only his own positive motivation to do the favor weighs in the balance. He doesn't (necessarily) take into account Alice's concerns (or put full weight on those concerns). So, to get the best possible equilibrium, Alice must punish Bob by some means if he fails to perform.[9]

The most obvious ways to add to Bob's motivation to fulfill his promise is, as in the story of Stiglitz and Kreps, to offer a combination of a cash "honorarium" if Bob performs—Alice offers to pay Bob $50 for driving her to the airport or $30 per hour spent helping her move or helping her study—and a cash "penalty" that he must pay Alice in the event of nonfulfillment. However, in the realm of social favors, such simple add-on motivations are rarely if ever seen. Why is that?

The simplest answer—if one is willing to go beyond "orthodox economics" and the *de gustibus* principle–is the Israeli day-care center story: imposing a financial penalty for nonperformance changes the character of the transaction, diminishing Bob's intrinsic motivation. If he has plenty of intrinsic motivation to begin with, adding on a penalty may be counterproductive.

And, as noted previously, other extrinsic incentives may be at work that supplement Bob's intrinsic motivation.

Back to Kreps and Stiglitz: suppose $H = P = 0$, and Kreps fails to show up. Stiglitz, presumably, will not invite Kreps to give any other talks. Kreps may offer an explanation for why he cannot show up, and Stiglitz's unhappiness may be tempered by a believable excuse. But it was within Kreps's ability to appear—he would have had to expend effort $\theta > B$ for the realized value of θ—and to increase Kreps's motivation to appear, Stiglitz may ex ante make it clear that if Kreps doesn't show, future invitations will not be forthcoming. Because (a priori) Kreps has an expected payoff of $3,657 for this sort of invitation, this will motivate Kreps to show beyond the immediate incentives he has, represented by B.

Moreover, individuals at Columbia will see that Kreps was a no-show. They may tell friends and associates. And, therefore, Kreps may find fewer invitations not only from Stiglitz but also from the wider community. Insofar as he attaches positive value to such invitations, this increases his motivation to appear.

Will the implicit "threat" of such punishment cause Kreps's intrinsic motivation to decrease in the way that a financial penalty might? Perhaps not. With $P = 0$, Kreps has a social obligation to appear. If his punishment for non-appearance is a social penalty, this is in keeping with his role (or identity) as a member of the community.

Assuming we accept the previous paragraph's contention, does this solve the problem and get us back to the first best? It may, if the punishment is only threatened and never triggered. But if there is positive probability that the punishment must and will be applied, it is inefficient. The punishment— Kreps misses out on future opportunities that he values—also involves a loss of payoff to those who would have invited him, insofar as they get positive payoffs from inviting Kreps, as is the case for this invitation from Stiglitz to Kreps. In other words, the punishment is dissipative—value is destroyed—and so, in theory and if it weren't that $P > 0$ affects Kreps's intrinisic motivation, such punishments are less efficient than the fully efficient imposition of a financial penalty. (Of course, this is based on the assumption of transferable payoff between Kreps and Stiglitz in the moment.)

What about the argument that Stiglitz won't mind destroying social value, as long as he can propose terms that make himself better off? Remember, in the numerical example, Stiglitz, on his own behalf, will happily impose a penalty of $P = \$30{,}000$, as long as doing so doesn't reduce Kreps's intrinsic motivation term to less than $17,000. A commonsense answer is that a proposal of this nature—come give a talk, and if you fail to show, pay me $30,000—is likely to trigger a reduction in intrinsic motivation much greater than a reduction of $3,000. Indeed, it may call forward other, more dramatic emotions on the part of the agent.

And this, I contend, is one reason we don't see social favors being "secured" by financial nonperformance penalties but, instead, by dissipative punishment. Insofar as Bob has intrinsic motivation not to fail Alice, whether taking her to the airport, or helping her move, or helping her prepare for an exam, and insofar as Alice saying "I'll only agree to accept your help if you agree to pay me a penalty if you fail" causes Bob's intrinsic motivation to decrease, Alice (and the community) do better to rely on Bob's intrinsic motivation, buttressed, perhaps, by the implicit threat of dissipative social punishment if Bob fails to come through.

HONORARIA WITHOUT A PENALTY

As noted at the start of the previous section, while penalties for nonperformance of social favors are something between rare and nonexistent, "honoraria" are in many cases common, aimed at the favor giver's participation constraint rather than her incentive constraint.

Suppose, for instance, that instead of the Arrow Lecture at Columbia University, the lecture in question is the Arrow Lecture at Cal State Ukiah (CSU).[10] Suppose the organizer at CSU, Daniel, very much wants to arrange for Carol, a renowned economist, to give the lecture. But Carol's B for giving a lecture as CSU is practically zero or even negative; the lecture is scheduled for January, so the chances of rain are very high. To attract Carol—that is, to satisfy her participation constraint—Daniel could offer a substantial honorarium H. But, as long as the support of θ extends beyond $B + H$, there is positive probability that Carol will fail to appear. And what is more important is that an honorarium alone cannot get Daniel and Carol to the social optimum; a penalty is required.

Concerning honoraria directed at the participation constraint, there is still an identity economics story to be told. When Alice asks Bob or several friends to help her move from her current residence to a new apartment, to induce them to agree she is less likely to offer them so many dollars per hour working for her than she is to say, "I'll provide pizza and beer." For social favors, "social" honoraria are more in keeping with the nature of the task.[11]

Finally, while I believe that honoraria are chiefly directed at participation, one can spin a story about how honoraria *enhance* intrinsic motivation: if Stiglitz offers Kreps an honorarium for the Arrow Lecture, perhaps this creates an intrinsic sense of obligation in Kreps; this lecture is important to Stiglitz, and Kreps doesn't wish to let him down. I pursue this story further in chapter 10.

9

THE QUALITY OF KREPS'S PERFORMANCE MATTERS AS WELL

It is fair, I think, to say that the qualitative point of the very simple models in the previous chapter is obvious, although the numbers in the example are striking. An elaboration on these models adds interest: suppose Kreps must expend effort not only to appear but also to present a high-quality lecture, and both Kreps's and Stiglitz's payoffs depend on the lecture's quality, assuming it is given.

We can use either variation of the formal model from chapter 8 to model this; I'll do one model for each, as they illustrate different points.

THE FIRST VARIATION

In the first model, Kreps's efforts all come a priori. Assume that his effort is two-dimensional: E is effort devoted to appearing, as before, and q is effort devoted to the quality of the lecture. The following pieces flesh out the model:

- Kreps's intrinsic motivation (assuming no honorarium or penalty) is $Bq^{1/2}$, which is realized only if he does in fact appear. That is, he has little motivation to present a poor model; his intrinsic motivation (satisfaction) rises with the quality of the talk he gives.
- Kreps appears with probability $\pi(E)$.
- Kreps's cost of preparing is $(E + 1)(q + 1) + k$. Please note that the mixed-partial on this cost term is strictly positive (is 1); more E raises the marginal cost of q and vice versa. (In a more general formulation, assume that the cost is $c(E, q)$ for a convex and strictly increasing function c with strictly positive mixed-partial derivatives [or, simply, increasing differences].)

Therefore, absent any honorarium H and no-show penalty P, Kreps chooses E and q to maximize

$$\pi(E)Bq^{1/2} - (E + 1)(q + 1) - k.$$

The first-order conditions (for an interior maximum) are

$$\pi'(E)Bq^{1/2} = q+1 \quad \text{and} \quad \pi(E)\frac{B}{2q^{1/2}} = E+1.$$

Solving this in closed form for a reasonable specification of π is beyond me, so I resort to numerical analysis: suppose

$$\pi(E) = 1 - e^{-0.00015E},\ B = \$40{,}000, \text{ and } k = \$10{,}000.$$

The optimized values for Kreps are

$$E = 5{,}840.25,\ q = 3.99, \text{ and } \pi(E) = 0.5835,$$

which gives Kreps an expected payoff of $7,479. However, because Kreps fails to arrive with probability in excess of 0.4, Stiglitz is very unhappy: if

- Stiglitz's dollar-denominated benefit if Kreps shows up with a talk of quality q is $\$10{,}000q^{1/2}$, and
- Stiglitz's embarrassment loss if Kreps fails to show up is a net loss of $20,000,

then Stiglitz's net expected payoff is only $3,331.75. To keep the exposition flowing smoothly, I assume that, in this example, Stiglitz's next best alternative gives him a payoff of $3,000, so he is barely willing to go with Kreps.[1]

As in chapter 8, Kreps is not taking into account the impact his decisions have on Stiglitz. Stiglitz would like to motivate Kreps both to increase the probability that he appears and to work harder at improving the quality of his talk. However, while Stiglitz has instruments—a combination of honorarium for appearance and penalty for non-appearance—to motivate Kreps to show up with greater probability, the subjective nature of "quality" makes it impossible for the two to draft an enforceable contract that is based on the quality of the talk Kreps delivers, if in fact he delivers a talk. This is a standard story in the branch of the principal-agent problem that deals with multitasking, so I take no more time to justify it.

Because Stiglitz can induce a higher probability of appearance, perhaps it is to his benefit to do so. Suppose he imposes a penalty of $10,000 if Kreps fails to show but offers no honorarium. And, for the moment, suppose that this has no impact on Kreps's intrinsic motivation. Then (solving numerically) Kreps appears with probability 0.657 with a talk of quality 3.47, which gives Kreps an expected payoff of \$3,645 and Stiglitz an expected payoff of \$8,534.

It is worth observing here that, just as in the models of chapter 8, combinations of H and P that hold $H + P$ constant provide the same choices by Kreps. Kreps chooses E and q to maximize

$$\begin{aligned}&\pi(E)[Bq^{1/2} + H] - (1 - \pi(E))P - (E + 1)(q + 1) - k \\ &= \pi(E)[Bq^{1/2} + H + P] - P - (E + 1)(q + 1) - k.\end{aligned}$$

The division of $H + P$ between H and P, as in previous models, simply redistributes payoff.

In terms of total expected payoff, the best sum of $H + P$ seems to be around \$21,000. See table 9.1 for values, where $H + P$ is configured entirely as a penalty for non-appearance.

Note that as the penalty increases, the probability that Kreps appears increases, and the quality of the talk he gives decreases. The second effect is the standard multitasking effect: the more incentive Kreps has to appear (to avoid paying the penalty), the more effort E he supplies to raise $\pi(E)$, which raises the marginal cost to him of effort devoted to quality of the talk and, therefore, the less quality effort he provides.[2] In fact, this is a bit more complex than the standard multitasking effect: in Kreps's objective function, the gain term is $\pi(E)Bq^{1/2}$, and, therefore, an increase in $\pi(E)$ increases the marginal benefit to him of higher-quality q. If the cross partial between π and q in the cost term was

Table 9.1 Finding the Socially Optimal $H + P$

Penalty	Sum of Expected Payoffs	Probability Kreps Appears	Quality of Kreps's Talk
\$15,000	\$12,484	0.670	3.24
\$18,000	\$12,572	0.690	3.12
\$19,000	\$12,587	0.695	3.08
\$20,000	\$12,596	0.700	3.04
\$21,000	\$12,598	0.704	3.01
\$22,000	\$12,594	0.709	2.97
\$24,000	\$12,569	0.720	2.90

Note: For the model as specified in the text, and assuming that the imposition of a penalty doesn't affect Kreps's intrinsic motivation, the table provides the impact of various values of $H + P$ (configured entirely as penalty) on Kreps's responses in terms of the sum of Kreps's and Stiglitz's expected payoffs, the probability Kreps appears, and the quality of the talk he gives. See the text for further commentary.

reduced—if, say, the cost term was $q + E + \kappa qE$ for small $\kappa > 0$—then increased incentive to appear would lead Kreps to increase his quality effort q.[3] But for the model with $\kappa = 1$, the cost cross-partial is (evidently) stronger than the benefit cross-partial.

THE FIRST VARIATION WITH CHILLED INTRINSIC MOTIVATION

The previous analysis assumes that Stiglitz can impose a penalty (or pay an honorarium, or both) with no impact on Kreps's intrinsic motivation. But, of course, the point here is to see what happens if the imposition of an honorarium and/

Table 9.2 Values if Imposing a Penalty Affects Kreps's Intrinsic Motivation commentary.

	Scenario 1	Scenario 2	Scenario 3	Scenario 4
ρ	1	1	0.9	0.5
H	\$0.00	\$0.00	\$5,000.00	\$0.00
P	\$0.00	\$21,000.00	\$16,000.00	\$21,000.00
E^*	5,840.25	8,125.74	8,090.50	7,886.30
q^* (quality of talk)	3.99	3.01	2.44	0.77
Probability Kreps appears	0.58	0.70	0.70	0.69
Kreps's expected payoff	\$7,479.39	\$90.74	\$450.34	−\$18,221.30
Stiglitz's expected payoff	\$3,331.73	\$12,507.75	\$6,286.93	\$6,406.26
Sum of payoffs	\$10,811.12	\$12,598.48	\$6,737.26	−\$11,815.05

Note: This table provides two scenarios in which Kreps's intrinsic motivation is lowered by 10 percent (scenario 3) and 50 percent (scenario 4) if Stiglitz imposes a penalty. See the text for further commentary.

or penalty decreases Kreps's intrinsic motivation. Because I cannot solve this model in closed form, we must be content with a few numbers, presented in table 9.2.

Scenario 1 is the baseline scenario, where $H = P = 0$. Scenario 2 assumes that Stiglitz can impose a penalty without affecting Kreps's intrinsic motivation; it gives fuller details from the line \$21,000 in table 9.1.

In scenarios 3 and 4, I suppose that imposing a penalty lowers Kreps's intrinsic motivation to $\rho Bq^{1/2}$ for $\rho = 0.9$ in scenario 3 and to $\rho = 0.5$ in scenario 4. In both scenarios, I assume $H + P = \$21{,}000$; in scenario 3, I distribute this as $H = \$5{,}000$ and $P = \$16{,}000$, so that Kreps's participation constraint is met by \$450 or so, while Stiglitz's participation constraint is very slack. But, in comparison with scenario 1, the sum of payoffs is decreased by more than \$4,000; if imposing a penalty sufficient to get Stiglitz's participation lowers Kreps's intrinsic motivation by 10 percent, the two are jointly worse off than with $H = P = 0$: with "all penalty," Stiglitz does better, but Kreps does worse by a greater amount. *Clearly, there is no way to reconfigure H and P such that $H + P = 21{,}000$ and, at the same time, to make both Kreps and Stiglitz better off than in the base case.*

This is the same effect as in chapter 8, but worse. What makes it worse is that by removing 10 percent of Kreps's intrinsic motivation and instead trying to motivate him to appear with a penalty, the quality of the talk he gives declines substantially, which is bad for both parties.

And, in scenario 4: if the imposition of a penalty causes Kreps's intrinsic motivation to halve, the sum of the expected payoffs (with $H + P = \$21{,}000$) is $-\$11{,}815.05$, largely because Kreps now prepares a terrible talk ($q^* = 0.77$). If this is the effect of imposing a penalty, the two obviously cannot come to a deal (with $P > 0$) that meets both participation constraints.[4]

Comparing scenarios 1 and 2, we see that if imposing a penalty doesn't lower Kreps's intrinsic motivation at all, the sum of expected payoffs goes up. However, scenario 3 shows that if imposing a penalty lowers Kreps's intrinsic motivation by 10 percent, this is worse in terms of the sum of payoffs than is $H = P = 0$. So, at what value of ρ can a penalty do just as well socially as $H = P = 0$? Because I'm solving this numerically, I can't give a precise answer. But if we fix $H + P = \$21{,}000$, the answer is approximately $\rho = 0.97$. In this model, if Kreps's intrinsic motivation is decreased by 3 percent or more with the imposition of a penalty, the two parties are jointly better off with $H = P = 0$.[5]

THE SECOND MODEL WITH QUALITY OF THE TALK

The second model of chapter 8 can also be adapted to incorporate the quality of Kreps's talk (if he gives it), given the incentives he faces.

Recall that, in the second model of chapter 8, "circumstances" θ resolve, allowing Kreps to decide whether to overcome them (and appear) or not. In this elaboration, he also decides, after observing θ, how much effort to devote to perfecting his talk, assuming he decides to give it. The cost of these efforts depends both on the quality q he chooses and the circumstances θ, given by a cost function $c(q; \theta)$. In line with the idea that choosing to show up under more adverse circumstance takes effort, $c(q; \theta)$ has a strictly positive mixed-partial derivative.

Prior to observing θ, Kreps makes initial efforts costing him k in preparing the talk. This term k includes some choice of pre-θ efforts devoted to the quality of the lecture. In this model, I assume that these efforts are fixed; the focus is on his decisions after observing θ.

In this formulation, given θ, and assuming that $H = P = 0$ for now, Kreps's net payoff if he chooses to appear is

$$B(q) - c(q; \theta) - k,$$

where B is strictly increasing and strictly concave. Therefore, *if Kreps chooses to appear*, he will present a talk of quality $q^*(\theta)$ where $q^*(\theta)$ satisfies

$$B'\left(q^*(\theta)\right) = \frac{\partial c\left(q^*(\theta), \theta\right)}{\partial q}.$$

Under the assumptions made, $q^*(\theta)$ is decreasing in θ; the harder it is to overcome the circumstances θ in order to appear, the lower are the efforts Kreps invests in the quality of the talk. Kreps's decision whether to appear is whether the post-θ cost of appearing is less than his intrinsic benefit from doing so; the cost k, being sunk, does not enter. That is, he appears for all θ such that

$$B(q^*(\theta)) \geq c(q^*(\theta); \theta).$$

Assuming that a single crossing holds, there is a cutoff value of θ, denoted θ^0, and Kreps's expected payoff is then

$$\int_0^{\theta^0} \left[B\left(q^*(\theta)\right) - c\left(q^*(\theta);\theta\right)\right] f(\theta)d\theta - k,$$

where f is the density function for the distribution of θ. In these circumstances, Stiglitz's ex ante expected utility is

$$\int_0^{\theta^0} \alpha\left(q^*(\theta)\right) f(\theta)d\theta - \left(1 - F\left(\theta^0\right)\right)\beta,$$

where $\alpha(q)$ is Stiglitz's dollar value for a talk of quality level q. As in the simpler model of the previous chapter, Kreps is not taking into account Stiglitz's interests, and Stiglitz may wish to try to motivate Kreps. And while (I assume) there is nothing Stiglitz can do to influence Kreps to increase q (for the same reasons as before), Stiglitz still can induce Kreps to put in more effort in making it to the talk, with an honorarium H if Kreps appears and a penalty P that Kreps must pay to Stiglitz if he (Kreps) is a no-show.

For the moment, assume that employing either or both of these two instruments has no impact on Kreps's intrinsic motivation, captured by the function B. How will a pair $H > 0$ and $P > 0$ affect Kreps's decisions? His post-θ payoff is $B(q) - c(q, \theta) + H - k$ if he chooses to appear and takes effort level q versus $-P - k$ if he does not. Because the honorarium is paid regardless of the quality of the talk, as long as it is given, Kreps's post-θ choice of quality, assuming he decides to appear, is the same, given by the same first-order equation. All that shifts is his decision whether to appear. Given θ, he chooses to appear if

$$B(q^*(\theta)) - c(q^*(\theta), \theta) + H \geq - P.$$

Still assuming a single crossing, let θ^1 be the solution to

$$B(q^*(\theta^1)) - c(q^*(\theta^1), \theta^1) + H + P = 0.$$

Of course, given the nature of the functions $\theta \to B(q^*(\theta))$ and $\theta \to c(q^*(\theta), \theta)$, this means $\theta^1 > \theta^0$. And because the quality of the talk, given θ, remains $q^*(\theta)$, *as long as Stiglitz prefers a talk of quality* $q^*(\theta^1)$ *to a no-show*—that is, as long as $\alpha(q^*(\theta^1)) > \beta$—Stiglitz is better off.

Is the first-best available? One must be careful in saying what this question means. In the truly efficient outcome, Kreps would internalize Stiglitz's enjoyment from a better lecture: in any state θ in which the lecture is given, q should be chosen to maximize $\alpha(q) + B(q) - c(q; \theta)$, hence he would choose $q^{\#}(\theta)$ that satisfies

$$\alpha'(q^{\#}(\theta)) + B'(q^{\#}(\theta)) = c'(q^{\#}(\theta); \theta).$$

But there is no instrument available (by assumption) that induces Kreps to choose q as a function of θ other than $q^*(\theta)$. However, what is "next best," if it is stipulated that Kreps chooses $q^*(\theta)$ given θ? Next best is to choose the cut-off value θ^0 to maximize

$$\int_0^{\theta^0} \left[B\left(q^*(\theta)\right)+\alpha\left(q^*(\theta)\right)-c\left(q^*(\theta);\theta\right)\right]f(\theta)d\theta-\left(1-F\left(\theta^0\right)\right)\beta,$$

and we get as first-order equation for the next-best

$$[B(q^*(\theta^0)) + \alpha(q^*(\theta^0)) - c(q^*(\theta^0); \theta^0)] + \beta = 0.$$

Hence, with no constraints on the signs of H and P, this next best is attained when

$$H + P = \alpha(q^*(\theta^0)) + \beta.$$

And, concerning Stiglitz's participation constraint, given H and P, his expected payoff with H and P is

$$\begin{aligned}
&\int_0^{\theta^0} \left[\alpha\left(q^*(\theta)\right)-H\right]f(\theta)d\theta-\left(1-F\left(\theta^0\right)\right)(\beta-P) \\
&=\int_0^{\theta^0} \left[\alpha\left(q^*(\theta)\right)-H+\beta-P\right]f(\theta)d\theta-\beta+P \\
&=\int_0^{\theta^0} \left[\alpha\left(q^*(\theta)\right)-\alpha\left(q^*\left(\theta^0\right)\right)\right]f(\theta)d\theta-\beta+P.
\end{aligned}$$

For this to exceed Stiglitz's reservation utility γ, we need

$$P \geq \beta + \gamma - \int_0^{\theta^0} \left[\alpha\left(q^*(\theta)\right) - \alpha\left(q^*\left(\theta^0\right)\right) \right] f(\theta) d\theta.$$

This is similar to what we had in chapter 8, where Stiglitz's participation in a (then) first-best scheme required $P \geq \beta + \gamma$. However, because Stiglitz benefits from the "surplus" he derives in terms of the quality of the talk for $\theta < \theta^0$, the penalty imposed on Kreps can be something less than $\beta + \gamma$.

WHAT HAPPENED TO "TRADITIONAL" MULTITASKING WOES?

In the first model of this chapter (where Kreps's effort choices are before he learns θ), the traditional multitasking effect was observed.[6] Here, though, this effect is missing. Having observed θ, Kreps must decide whether he will appear or not. And, only then, he decides how much quality to put into the talk, where the strictly positive mixed-second partial implies that larger θ goes with lower q, *regardless of whether he is motivated to appear because of his intrinsic motivation or because of a combination of that intrinsic motivation and an honrorarium/penalty laid on top.* In this sense, the current formulation isolates our analysis from the traditional multitasking story.

I do not say that the traditional multitasking issue is unimportant. A better, more complex model would mix the two models, with Kreps taking steps before the realization of θ both to enhance the probability that he can appear and to prepare a high-quality talk and then, as circumstances resolve, asking himself (a) whether it is worth pushing through and (b) how much fine-tuning effort to provide. However, isolating from the standard multitasking issue focuses attention on context.

HONORARIA AND/OR PENALTIES REDUCE KREPS'S INTRINSIC MOTIVATION

The next step is, I expect, obvious. We posit that Stiglitz can propose an honorarium H and a penalty P, but doing so reduces Kreps's intrinsic motivation. Therefore, by doing this, Stiglitz faces a double whammy: reducing Kreps's intrinsic motivation means, ceteris paribus, that he appears in fewer states θ. Ceteris is, of course, not paribus, because the imposition of H and P will move the cutoff value of θ in the other direction; it is the trade-off between these two forces that is the issue.

But, in addition, lowering Kreps's intrinsic motivation also results in less polishing effort. This is unambiguous. Stiglitz has no tools at his disposal to motivate greater effort at increasing the quality of the talk.

To illustrate, I'll present a numerical example. Things are not so easy as in the previous chapter, and so a closed-form solution is not possible. (The problem is in evaluating the integrals that give Kreps's and Stiglitz's payoffs.)

- As before, θ's distribution function is $F(\theta) = 1 - e^{-\lambda\theta}$ for $\lambda = 0.00015$. This means the average value of θ is 6,666.67, and Kreps appears with probability 0.95 if he appears whenever $\theta \le 20{,}000$.

- For Kreps's initial intrinsic-motivation term (absent any honorarium or penalty), set $B(q) = \$10{,}000q^{1/2}$. If Stiglitz imposes a penalty, Kreps's intrinsic motivation term scales down to $\$10{,}000\rho q^{1/2}$ for a parameter ρ to be varied in various scenarios.
- Kreps's initial cost is $k = \$5k$.
- Kreps's follow-on cost function is $c(\theta, q) = 2{,}500(\theta/20{,}000 + 1)q + \theta/4$.

Hence, if Kreps chooses to appear in the face of difficulty θ, he selects q to maximize

$$10{,}000\rho q^{1/2} - 2{,}500(\theta/20{,}000 + 1)q,$$

which gives the first-order condition

$$\frac{10{,}000\rho}{2q^{1/2}} = 2{,}500(\theta/20{,}000 + 1)$$

$$\text{and, therefore,} \quad q^*(\theta) = \frac{4\rho^2}{(\theta/20{,}000 + 1)^2}.$$

This gives a rather dramatic change in the quality of Kreps's talk as a function of θ: for $\rho = 1$, $q^*(0) = 4$, while $q^*(20{,}000) = 1$. For $\rho = 0.5$, $q^*(0) = 1$, and $q^*(20{,}000) = 0.25$.

- Continuing the formulation, Stiglitz's benefit function is $\alpha(q) = \$7{,}500 \times q^{1/2}$, his loss from non-appearance by Kreps is $\beta = \$20{,}000$, and his reservation payoff is \$7,000.

To find the expected payoffs for Kreps and Stiglitz in the scenario at a given H, P, and ρ, we first must compute the cutoff value of θ for Kreps. His net benefit from appearing, for a given θ, is

$$10{,}000\rho q^*(\theta)^{1/2} + H + P,$$

while the cost to him of appearing is

$$2{,}500(\theta/20{,}000 + 1)q^*(\theta) + \theta/4,$$

where I've included the penalty amount P among the benefits to him, as the decision to appear saves him from paying the penalty. Hence his cutoff θ, as a function of H, P, and ρ, is where

$$\begin{aligned}&10{,}000\rho q^*(\theta)^{1/2} + H + P\\ &= 2{,}500(\theta/20{,}000 + 1)q^*(\theta) + \theta/4,\end{aligned}$$

assuming single crossing. Substituting in $q^*(\theta)$, this is

$$\begin{aligned}&10{,}000\rho\frac{2\rho}{(\theta/20{,}000+1)} + H + P\\ &= 2{,}500(\theta/20{,}000+1)\frac{4\rho^2}{(\theta/20{,}000+1)^2} + \frac{\theta}{4},\end{aligned}$$

which simplifies to

$$\frac{10{,}000\rho^2}{(\theta/20{,}000+1)} + H + P = \frac{\theta}{4}.$$

With this formula, we are clear that single crossing holds.[7] Also, note that k is a a sunk cost and so doesn't enter into Kreps's decision, having observed θ, whether to press on.

It remains to find the expected payoffs for Kreps and Stiglitz and then to compare the base case $H = P = 0$ with "optimal" levels of H and P for different values of ρ. Because the expected payoffs involve very messy integrals, I resort at this point to numerical analysis; see table 9.3.

There are several points to make about this model and table 9.3.

Table 9.3 The Second Model with Quality of the Talk

	Scenario 1	Scenario 2	Scenario 3	Scenario 4	Scenario 5
ρ	1	1	0.9	0.8	0.5
H	$0.00	$0.00	$300.00	$1,620.00	$4,700.00
P	$0.00	$17,000.00	$16,700.00	$15,800.00	$13,300.00
Probability that Kreps appears	0.95	>0.999976	>0.999976	>0.999976	>0.999976
Average quality of talk conditional on appearance	2.67	2.576	2.086	1.648	0.644
Kreps's expected payoff	$1,338.00	$1,224.00	$27.62.00	$8.26.00	$15.61.00
Stiglitz's expected payoff	$10,496.00	$11,817.00	$10,336.00	$7,834.00	$1,209.00
Sum of expected payoffs	$11,834.00	$13,041.00	$10,364.00	$7,842.00	$1,225.00

Note: See the text for further commentary.

The probability of Kreps appearing in all scenarios except scenario 1 is " >0.99976." This is because, in the numerical analysis, I stopped at $\theta = 74{,}100$, and $1 - e^{-0.00015 \times 74{,}100} = 0.99976$. That is, in all the $P > 0$ scenarios, P was chosen so that Kreps would definitely appear.

And, for these values, having Kreps appear for all $\theta \leq 74{,}100$ is both optimal for Stiglitz and socially. In fact, in this model, Stiglitz wants Kreps to appear: as long as the quality of the talk is ≥ 0, Stiglitz gets additional benefit (and avoids the \$20,000 cost of embarrassment) if Kreps shows up.

Contrast this with the first model of this chapter: there, when Stiglitz introduces a penalty, Kreps increases E, which decreases the quality of his talk; Stiglitz, therefore, is balancing increasing the probability of Kreps showing up with the quality of the talk Kreps gives. In this model, Kreps *decides* whether to show up (based on his incentives) and, when and if he decides to appear, he chooses the quality solely based on θ. So here, unlike in the first model, once Stiglitz decides to impose a penalty, he "goes all the way" and chooses H and P to ensure that Kreps appears. It would be interesting to look at a model where, if the quality of talk is poor enough, Stiglitz would rather that Kreps not show up.

And, for this model, Kreps's cost of preparing the talk (at his optimal level of quality given ρ and θ) is never more than \$20,000, for $\theta \leq 74{,}100$. Therefore, from a social point of view, Kreps should always appear, to spare Stiglitz from his \$20,000 embarrassment.

However, if in this model we went far beyond $\theta = 74{,}100$ or if we put in place a model in which there are qualities that are worse for Stiglitz than non-appearance, there can be a difference between the set of states θ for which Stiglitz wants kreps to appear and those for which Kreps should appear, to maximize the sum of their expected payoffs.

As always, Kreps's motivation to appear depends on $H + P$ and not how the sum is split between penalty and honorarium. But as ρ declines, it takes a larger $H + P$ to induce Kreps to appear for all $\theta \leq 74{,}100$.

In the fashion of earlier models, as Kreps is less intrinsically motivated, the sum of payoffs declines. If $\rho = 1$—that is, the imposition of a penalty doesn't affect Kreps's intrinsic motivation, which is scenario 2—then the sum of payoffs exceeds the base case, although the average quality of the talk declines, because it averages in states with bigger θs, which means lower $q^*(\theta)$.[8]

However, as ρ declines, the quality of Kreps's talk declines in all states θ, lowering the sum of payoffs. In scenarios 3, 4, and 5, H and P are chosen just to meet Kreps's participation constraint, and even when $\rho = 0.9$, Stiglitz, while holding Kreps to near his participation constraint value of \$0, is worse off than in the base case. In this model, if $\rho < 0.955$, the sum of expected payoffs is less than the base case, although for some values of ρ close to and below 0.955, Stiglitz can improve his own expected payoff by imposing a penalty and "draining" surplus from Kreps.

THE POWER OF SOCIAL PUNISHMENT

In chapter 8, the idea was advanced that, instead of motivating Kreps through financial rewards and penalties, a "social" penalty might be used. The disadvantage of a social penalty—Kreps is punished by withdrawing invitations for a while in the future—is that it is dissipative. But, insofar as Kreps regards this as a "social penalty for social malfeasance"—a punishment that fits the crime—the prospect of such a punishment might not change the nature of the transaction and, therefore, might not reduce (or reduce as much) Kreps's intrinsic motivation to appear.

To this advantage a second can now be added: Kreps and Stiglitz, we assume, cannot contract on the quality of Kreps's talk; quality is subjective, and if Stiglitz were to demand a financial penalty from Kreps, saying "You gave a poor talk," Kreps would rejoin, "No, it was a very fine talk. I'm not paying." Insofar as the talk is before an audience, however, Stiglitz can grumble to his colleagues afterward, "That was not very good." And his colleagues, if they agree, might relay this information to others in the profession, leaving Kreps without opportunities to give other talks. Kreps, aware that his reputation as the giver of good talks is on the line, is extrinsically motivated to preserve that reputation. And, insofar as this doesn't adversely impact his intrinsic motivation for this particular talk, it is all good.

BOTTOM LINE?

I think the bottom line from these models with a quality dimension is obvious. Insofar as quality of a social favor matters, insofar as Alice can reward and/or penalize Bob on the basis of whether he does the favor but *not* on how well he does it, and insofar as Bob has intrinsic motivation to do a good job that might be chilled if monetary incentives for did/did not performance are applied, then Alice may be well off avoiding the imposition of those monetary incentives.

10

INTRINSIC MOTIVATION TO DO WHAT, EXACTLY?

However, . . .

In the models of chapters 8 and 9, Kreps's intrinsic motivation was qualitatively aligned with Stiglitz's desires. In chapter 8, Stiglitz wants Kreps to appear; Kreps must consider the cost of doing so, but in terms of intrinsic motivation, he only gets the benefit B if he does so. In chapter 9, Stiglitz wants a high-quality talk; Kreps's benefit only accrues if he appears and is larger the higher is the quality of his talk; and the two agree (at least ordinally) on what constitutes high(er) quality.

But in other cases—in other models one can construct, as well as in real-life employment contexts—the intrinsic motivation of the agent does not align qualitatively with the interests of the principal. Here are two real-life examples.

ENGINEERS WORKING FOR HIGH-TECH START-UPS

From roughly 1995 until 2000, my colleagues James Baron, Diane Burton, and Michael Hannan studied a sample of around 150 high-tech start-ups in and around Silicon Valley, categorizing their human-resource-management blueprints according to the founders' visions, and then tracking how those blueprints evolved as the companies grew (or not) and how the companies fared in terms of financial performance.[1] They characterized the blueprints on the basis of the answers to three questions:

1. What is the basis of attachment and retention of key technical employees? Companies were sorted into three buckets: compensation; employee attachment to the work itself; attachment to the group as a community.
2. How were key technical employees selected? Buckets were: based on their skills; exceptional talent/potential; and fit with the organization's community.
3. What was the means of control and coordination of key technical employees? Buckets were: direct monitoring; peer/cultural control; reliance on standards of the profession; formal processes and procedures.

This gives 3 × 3 × 4 = 36 possible "blueprints," but the authors found that, in their sample of firms, most clustered into one of five paradigmatic organization types: star organizations; engineering organizations; commitment organizations; bureaucracies; and autocracies.

Of interest in the current context are star-model organizations, which selected key employees based on their exceptional potential, retained them by allowing employees to do work that the employees wanted to do, and controlled behavior by professional norms. In terms of financial performance, star-model organizations were overall mediocre, but if you restrict attention to firms that reached IPO, those star-model organizations that did reach IPO performed exceptionally well (compared to other forms that reached IPO).

The data aren't rich enough to test seriously the following story, but they are consistent with it: star-model organizations foster a culture of (what else?) stars, individual technical employees who absolutely excel as individuals. Such individuals, the story goes, are intrinsically motivated to achieve technical perfection. But technical perfection is not necessarily congruent with economic success; the adage "the perfect is the enemy of the good" applies. Hence, *if* these organizations made it to IPO, with a "perfect product" that also met the market test, they would do exceptionally well. But over the broader sample, the attempt to be "perfect" would chew up resources and might never reach a stage where the market would respond positively.

Admittedly, this story is a large leap from the data.[2] A sample of 150 firms is exceptional in this sort of organizational sociology. But when one looks at the organizations classified as "stars," they constituted only 10 percent of the sample, and only a subset of those made it to IPO. And the study didn't seek direct information about the intrinsic motivation of the star performers.

Still, the point is: in a star-model organization, a technical star may well be intrinsically motivated to exhibit her star quality, which is not necessarily aligned with what management and investors would prefer in terms of bringing a product to market.

PRIMARY NURSING AT BETH ISRAEL HOSPITAL

From around 1970 until 2000, nursing at Beth Israel Hospital in Boston was organized in a system called *primary nursing*. In this system, senior RNs (registered nurses) would serve as primary nurses to patients, with each primary nurse holding a caseload of around three patients at any one time. A patient's primary nurse was responsible for coordinating the patient's care: doctors would work through a patient's primary nurse rather than a "head nurse" in a ward or floor. A patient's primary nurse, during her 8-hour shift, would tend to all her patient's needs (unless occupied with another of her patients), including "menial" tasks such as bathing patients, emptying bed pans, and changing bed linen. (Such "menial" tasks are left to more junior nurses or nurse's aides, in the usual manner of organizing the nursing function.) And, in the 16 hours she was off duty, a patient's primary nurse was still "on call"; if one of her patients had a crisis, she would be called; if the family of a patient wanted to talk about what was going on, she would be called. All in all, this gave primary nurses much more work and much more responsibility. But their compensation was not increased.

The motivation for adopting this system was a belief on the part of the head of the hospital, Dr. Mitchell Rabkin, that nurses possess a lot of information about patients; Dr. Rabkin wished to activate that information. Doctors at Beth Israel were at first skeptical, but they quickly came to appreciate that this elevation in the status and importance of RNs resulted in better information for them and better care for their patients. Patients loved the system; Beth Israel became known throughout Boston as the best hospital in Boston to be a patient if, God forbid, you had to go into a hospital.

And the senior RNs loved the system. The social-psychology theory known as self-determination theory holds that employee intrinsic motivation is enhanced if the employee (a) has greater autonomy, (b) has greater opportunities to use and exhibit her skills, (c) has closer human contact with others, and (d) has a greater sense of purpose.[3] (Translating this well-established theory of motivation from social psychology into the terminology of identity economics is obvious.) The theory fits perfectly with primary nursing, and, indeed, with no more compensation on offer, primary nurses were motivated to work better and harder and exhibited greater job satisfaction and lower turnover. Moreover, nurses from other Boston hospitals queued up to get jobs at Beth Israel.

Finally, health-care outcomes improved. This was a win for all concerned: doctors, patients, nurses, and the hospital, the reputation of which grew in consequence.

However, by 2000, changes in how hospitals were compensated had shifted from fee-for-service to so-called diagnosis-resource-group (DRG) compensation, in which a set amount is paid to the hospital based on the patient's initial diagnosis, and even capitation, in which the hospital is paid a fixed annual fee to provide care for a patient. Primary nursing builds a very strong and personal bond between a senior RN and "her" patients. That bond—item (c) in the list of characteristics of self-determination theory—is an important driver of the intrinsic motivation of senior RNs. But it raises the possibility that senior RNs overprescribe services, including length of stay, for their patients. For a hospital compensated by insurance companies (including Medicaid/Medicare) on a fee-for-service basis, this does not present a significant problem. But, with DRG compensation and capitation, a senior RN's intrinsic motivation, as created in the primary-nursing practice, comes into conflict with the financial necessities of the hospital.[4]

CAN EXTRINSIC REWARDS ENHANCE INTRINSIC MOTIVATION?

Return to the story of Kreps and Stiglitz. In chapter 9, the quality of the talk was one-dimensional, and Kreps and Stiglitz agreed that "more" along that dimension was a good thing. But suppose talks have two dimensions of quality: technical complexity (that is, a lot of very impressive but abstruse mathematics) and broad appeal to economists in general. Suppose Kreps is intrinsically motivated to provide technical complexity, while Stiglitz is interested in a talk that will appeal to all his colleagues.

If the only instruments that Stiglitz has with which to influence Kreps are H and P, it would seem that he may be stuck with the talk that Kreps is motivated to prepare. However, these are not the only instruments at Stiglitz's disposal: Just as the threat of "social punishment" might be effective (if inefficient in application) in getting Kreps to appear, and just as the threat of this form of punishment might induce greater quality effort from Kreps (while H and P are ineffective), so the threat of this form of punishment might shift Kreps to take into account Stiglitz's interests in a general-appeal talk:

as long as Stiglitz makes clear to Kreps that he and his colleagues are looking for a general-appeal talk and not some mathematical gobbledygook, Kreps understands that a technically sophisticated talk might lead to fewer invitations in the future, both at Columbia and, through the power of the grapevine, at other institutions as well, as long as those other institutions are also looking for speakers with general appeal.

This is, of course, purely extrinsic incentive. But is it possible for Stiglitz to use the instruments he has at hand to shift Kreps's intrinsic motivation? Suppose that Stiglitz (a) offers Kreps an unconditional honorarium for accepting the invitation—at the extreme, an honorarium that Kreps receives even if he fails to appear—and, at the same time, (b) makes clear that he wants a talk with general appeal. Might this unconditional honorarium create a sense of intrinsic obligation in Kreps to provide Stiglitz with the sort of talk he (Stiglitz) wants? To be clear, I'm not suggesting that Kreps is more inclined to provide a general-appeal talk because it increases the chanced of future, similar honoraria. The story here is that, even if this is a once-in-a-lifetime invitation, and Kreps is aware that it is once-in-a-lifetime, the honorarium—the *unconditional* honorarium—can create this sense of obligation to "earn" it on the terms on which it was offered.

The point is that the meme—extrinsic rewards crowd out intrinsic motivation—is insufficiently nuanced. If the extrinsic rewards align with some form of intrinsic incentive, they can strengthen that intrinsic incentive. An example was provided in chapter 4: stock options for employees. Recall the argument: for some employees—the CEO and other members of the C-suite—stock options can conceivably make purely economic sense as an incentive device. But for most other employees, the level of risk in this form of compensation is way out of balance with the control most employees have over the fortunes of the company. However, if an employee, in possession of stock options, considers herself as an owner or team member rather than "just" an employee, the employee, with a feeling of responsibility for the organization, may provide a consummate effort on behalf of "her" company.

Another example from social psychology and organizational behavior goes by the rubric "gift exchange."[5] In the context of employment, the norm of reciprocity holds that, if the employee feels that the company for which she works is doing favors for her, she is obligated to reciprocate. Gift exchange refines this general notion by describing what sorts of gifts are most effective in triggering the norm of reciprocity: gifts are more effective the more they are personalized to the employee and the more they are perceived as provided through personal efforts by the boss. So, for instance, if Alice has performed particularly well in her job, to encourage further such efforts, her boss might reward her with, say, an all-expenses-paid weekend for Alice and her partner. An orthodox economist would claim that it makes more sense for the employer to give Alice the equivalent amount of cash to spend as she likes. But (and ignoring tax considerations), a psychologist would claim that, to motivate further "gifts" to the organization from Alice, the personalized gift can be more effective.

11

INTERNALIZATION OF THE OTHER PARTY'S WELFARE

When it comes to intrinsic motivation in a relationship, perhaps the best (in terms of getting closer to an efficient outcome) is if each party internalizes the welfare of the other party. Suppose, for instance, that Kreps, in addition to his intrinsic motivation to give a high-quality Arrow Lecture, also internalizes Stiglitz's welfare. Any of the models constructed previously will do; I'll use the second model from chapter 9. Suppose that Stiglitz has no concern for Kreps's welfare.[1] Stiglitz's personal-concerns utility is as before: $u_S = U_S$ is given by $7{,}500q^{1/2}$ if Kreps gives a talk of quality q, and $-20{,}000$ if he is a no-show. Kreps's own personal-concerns utility u_K is given by $10{,}000q^{1/2} - c(\theta,q) - 5{,}000$ if he shows and gives a talk of quality q when "circumstances" are θ, and $-5{,}000$ if he chooses not to show.

This does not fully describe Kreps's utility function, however. In the spirit of the model introduced in chapter 3, Kreps's "greater-concerns" utility function is this personal-concerns utility plus k times Stiglitz's personal-concerns utility; that is, Kreps chooses his actions on the basis of the overall utility function U_K, given by

$$(10{,}000 + 7{,}500k)q^{1/2} - c(\theta, q) - 5{,}000$$

if he shows, and $-5{,}000 - 20{,}000k$ if he fails to show. As before, $c(\theta, q) = 2{,}500(\theta/20{,}000 + 1)q + \theta/4$. Kreps's reservation level of utility for initial acceptance is interesting; before it was zero, but now Kreps internalizes Stiglitz's utility. If, say, Stiglitz's best alternative gives him (Stiglitz) utility level 7,000, to be consistent, Kreps should require an overall utility level of 7,000k to accept.

Suppose Kreps accepts initially and observes θ. His optimal choice of q, if he chooses to go, is

$$q^*(\theta) = \left(\frac{40{,}000 + 30{,}000k}{\theta + 20{,}000} \right)^2.$$

And Kreps chooses to go, once he observes θ, if

$$(10{,}000 + 7{,}500k)q^*(\theta)^{1/2} - \left[2{,}500\left(\frac{\theta}{20{,}000} + 1 \right) q^*(\theta) + \frac{\theta}{4} \right] > -20{,}000k.$$

For his acceptance of the initial offer, numerical integration is required.

Before providing some numbers, it is worth observing that this internalization of Stiglitz's welfare has three significant effects:

1. For any given θ, $q^*(\theta)$ will increase in k.
2. And, because Kreps's intrinsic motivation to give a good talk increases in k, he is more likely to appear.
3. Moreover, Kreps suffers along with Stiglitz if he doesn't show up, which increases even further the range of θ for which he chooses to appear.

And, in addition, Kreps's enjoyment of Stiglitz's enjoyment will mean that his welfare, measured in dollars, will increase quite significantly. (But see the following for a qualification to this statement.)

Table 11.1 records what happens in this model, assuming $H = P = 0$, for $k = 0.1$ to 0.5. The numbers speak for themselves.

Suppose that Stiglitz, by imposing a penalty, does not in the least affect Kreps's intrinsic motivation, which is based on honoring Arrow and enjoying the hospitality of Columbia, but this does kill completely Kreps's internalization of

Table 11.1 Kreps Also Internalizes Stiglitz's Welfare

	$k = 0$	$k = 0.1$	$k = 0.2$	$k = 0.3$	$k = 0.4$	$k = 0.5$
Probability that Kreps appears	0.95	0.9838	0.9948	0.9984	0.9995	0.9998
Average quality of the talk	2.67	3.015	3.421	3.870	4.355	4.870
Stiglitz's expected payoff	\$10,496	\$12,283	\$13,460	\$14,437	\$15,352	\$16,246
Kreps's expected payoff	\$1,338	\$2,518	\$3,796	\$5,181	\$6,665	\$8,242

Note: See the text for explanation.

Stiglitz's welfare. If $k = 0$ (Kreps puts no weight on Stiglitz's welfare), the best Stiglitz can do with an H and a P is to get \$13,041 for himself (and this involves a negative honorarium!). The numbers work out so that, if $k \geq 0.162$, Stiglitz does better with $P = 0$.

Consider, however, the possibility that, if Stiglitz offers Kreps an honorarium but with no penalty, this will enhance Kreps's sense of obligation to Stiglitz, in effect increasing k. I won't bore you with the numbers, but it should be clear from the numbers in table 11.1 that this could be fruitful for Stiglitz. But, if you try to do the calculations, one point should be watched. Suppose Stiglitz offers Kreps an honorarium of \$5,000. Suppose Kreps's k, in consequence, rises from (say) 0.1 to 0.2. Because Stiglitz is out-of-pocket \$5,000 and $k = 0.2$, Kreps "codes" his honorarium as only being \$4,000; he feels badly about the \$5,000 reduction (more or less, if the honorarium is contingent on appearing) in Stiglitz's wallet.[2]

Once again, the bottom line is obvious. If agent A internalizes the welfare of principal B, A's efforts on B's behalf will improve, the more so the stronger is A's internalization of B's welfare. Hence, B incurs lower "agency costs." The increase we see in the example in Kreps's payoff as k increases, on the other hand, is something of an apples-and-oranges comparison; Kreps with $k = 0.1$ is different from Kreps with $k = 0.2$, and comparing their payoffs is less legitimate.

And, moreover, return to the story in which Kreps's non-internalization intrinsic motivation is to give a highly technical talk, while Stiglitz prefers a talk that is aimed more at a general audience. Suppose this is a matter of degree. And suppose Kreps also internalizes Stiglitz's welfare. Then, it is clear, the more Kreps internalizes Stiglitz's welfare, the less technical will be the talk he provides. I won't bother providing indicative numbers from the formal model; this is patently obvious.

"TRADING FAVORS" WHEN ONE PARTY INTERNALIZES THE WELFARE OF THE OTHER PARTY

I contend that, when it comes to efficiency in relationships, an important element is the extent to which one party does "voluntary" favors for the other. Economic theory models the provision of such favors—and the motivation behind their provision—as follows.

Alice and Bob are engaged in a long-term relationship. At random times, the opportunity arrives for one of the two parties to do a favor for the other party; think of exponential interarrival times or, in discrete time with very short real time between epochs, a small probability of an arrival in each period. The opportunity may be for Alice to do a favor for Bob; it may run the other way around. Each favor comes with a cost incurred by the favor giver and a benefit to the favor receiver, if the favor is done. If favors arrive frequently enough, relative to the rate at which the parties discount streams of payoffs, and if the succession of favor opportunities is "balanced" in the sense that Alice has frequent enough opportunities to do favors for Bob and vice versa, then an equilibrium is possible in which a selection of these favors is done, based on the prospect of reciprocity (or, rather, the threat of a breakdown of reciprocity). The equilibrium could be an all-favors equilibrium, if the largest cost of any favor isn't large relative to the loss of future favors; or, more efficiently, it could involve a selection of those favors whose benefit to the receiver outweighs its cost.[3]

And, in a larger "community" setting, even if Alice's and Bob's opportunities to do favors for each other are infrequent when measured against the discount rate, one can rely on community enforcement of favor giving, as long as each party has frequent enough opportunities to do favors for some other member of the group and frequent enough opportunities to have a favor done for them, as long as the community as a whole observes when opportunities for favor giving arrive and, then, whether the favor is granted. (Think of the "community" here as a cohesive work group or an extended family.)

From the perspective of creating efficient equilibria, the ideal is where both Alice and Bob or, in the setting of community enforcement, every member of the community observes the possibility of each favor, its cost, its benefit, and whether it is ultimately done. But this ideal does not always describe reality:

- Even in the bilateral case of Alice and Bob, when Alice has an opportunity to do a favor for Bob, its cost to her may be known only to her (not to Bob), and its benefit to him may be private information to him. Perhaps the all-favors equilibrium still exists, if the average cost of a favor is less than the average benefit, the maximum cost is bounded, and the discount factor (measured in terms of the average time between favor opportunities) is close enough to 1. And, one can construct selection-of-favors equilibria, where Alice (say) refuses to do a favor for Bob if she learns privately that it is very costly. But, if Alice refuses to do a favor on the grounds of its private cost to her, she must pay some price for this; otherwise, she would always claim that every favor is prohibitively costly. One equilibrium construction has Bob released from the obligation to do the next favor (or some number of favors) for Alice that comes along.

- A more complex equilibrium construction found in the literature involves a supply of imaginary "tokens" that circulate between Alice and Bob: if an opportunity for Alice to do a favor comes along, and if she holds some subset of these tokens, she can demur, but doing so debits her token account by one and adds one to Bob's account. If she has no tokens in her account, then (in equilibrium) she is obligated to do all favors, unless and until Bob demurs from doing her a favor, which provides her account with a token. Each party, then, faced with a costly favor, must decide whether to spend a token (if the party has at least one) on this favor or to save it for some future, even costlier favor. Phrases such as "I (Alice) have a net positive balance in our relationship, Bob, on which I am drawing" is (at least to the theorist) formalized by such a token-based equilibrium.
- In the case of community enforcement, perhaps the favor giver and favor receiver know the cost and benefit, but the wider community doesn't have this information; the wider community only sees when a favor opportunity arises and, if so, whether it is done. This opens a possibility in which the favor receiver can offer a public excuse ("Alice doesn't need to do this favor for me") or

public forgiveness ("I don't mind that Alice failed to do this favor for me"); see Bowen, Kreps, and Skrzypacz for analysis of equilibria in such circumstances.[4]

- We already discussed the possibility that, between the time the favor is requested and when it is to be granted, the cost to the favor giver may unexpectedly rise, and the favor giver may wish to break an earlier promise to grant the favor. This would not be a problem, necessarily, if the favor receiver understands how expensive the cost of the favor has become. But this information is not always available to both sides.

And consider the following more complex yet real-life possibilities, both set in the context of a bilateral relationship.

- Suppose Alice sees when she has the opportunity to do something nice for Bob, but Bob is unaware of this unless and until Alice does the favor.
- Or imagine that, on occasion, Alice has the opportunity to do something nice for Bob, but, if she does, Bob is unaware that Alice was his benefactor or, perhaps, even that someone went out of their way to improve his well-being.

I am unaware of any models of these last two situations. If "daylight favors"—those where both parties are aware of the favor opportunity—are frequent enough, we can construct an equilibrium in which the last two types of favor are never done on the basis of a principle of "no (apparent) harm, no foul." But, of course, a loss of efficiency is entailed. And, while more complex, we might imagine equilibria where some of the "favors done partly in the dark"—where Bob realizes that Alice did something nice for him—can be done. For instance, we might imagine, in a token-style equilibrium, that Bob surrenders a token to Alice if she does such a favor for him (although, to keep her from doing menial favors simply to earn a token, it must be common knowledge between the two parties when the favor is of significant value or involves significant cost). Harder still is to imagine why Alice would do favors for Bob that are completely in the dark; that is, favors for which Bob isn't aware that Alice or even anyone was his benefactor.

I appreciate that I'm going on at great length concerning variations on the basic favor-trading model in which, because of informational infirmities, some socially efficient favors are likely to go undone. But—to come finally to the point—all the standard models, and all the variations about which I speculate, are based on selfish behavior by Alice and by Bob; they will only do a favor for another party if, in prospect, there will be some return for them. And that is not, necessarily, human nature.

Arrow suggests one "mechanism" by which such favors may be done: suppose Alice truly enjoys—has intrinsic motivation for—doing favors for others; doing them gives her a "warm glow."[5] Another mechanism is when, in a society, there is a norm of doing favors, and Alice (and Bob) are hardwired—have intrinsic motivation for—living up to the norms of their society. These are both important mechanisms; see, for instance, Bowles and Gintis.[6]

But it should be obvious that a third—and I think important—mechanism is if Alice and Bob, by virtue of their long relationship, internalize each other's welfare. A formal model is probably unnecessary, but just to nail down the idea: if Alice attaches weight 0.2 to Bob's welfare (in a dollar-denominated utility function), and if the opportunity for her to do a favor for him that costs her $10 and, she estimates, provides him with $100 in benefit, then doing the favor improves her greater utility by $10; she does it.

And please note: even in the full-information trading-favors game, if Alice internalizes Bob's welfare in this fashion, the balance of favors that she will do for him shifts toward "more favors." I forbear from saying this leads to a more efficient relationship for reasons given earlier in this chapter: welfare comparisons of Alice and Bob's relationship when Alice has no regard for Bob's welfare versus when she does involve comparing apples with oranges: Alice who cares about Bob's welfare is a different person from Alice who doesn't.[7] Still, Alice doing more favors for Bob can have dynamic consequences.

Which leads me, finally, to the dynamic story that, in my opinion, is the final nail in the coffin of Becker's admonition that prenups should be made mandatory.

12

DYNAMICS BASED ON BEM'S SELF-PERCEPTION THEORY

The story is simple. Alice is married to Pat but without a detailed contract signed at the inception of the marriage. As time passes, Alice has the opportunity, at some personal cost, to do things that will improve Pat's welfare. Some of these opportunities involve favors done partly in the dark—Pat won't know about them unless and until Alice does them—and some will be completely in the dark, meaning that Pat won't ever realize that Alice did them; she'll only know that good things happened for her. Moreover, most favor possibilities involve a degree of quality that is at the discretion of the favor giver.

Early on in the marriage, Alice does these favors for Pat and does them well, because (say) she is deeply in the throes of romantic love. Having done so, in accordance with self-perception theory, Alice asks herself the question, "Why?" She sets on the explanation that it is out of love and regard for Pat and, per self-perception theory, this is built into her perception of who she is or reinforces this perception in her, which enhances (or, at least, maintains) her willingness to do favors for Pat and to do them well. A virtuous cycle ensues.

Of course, Alice anticipates that Pat will reciprocate, and one could explain her behavior at least in part as an orthodox Nash equilibrium of a "standard trading-favors" game. I don't dispute that this enters into it. But, especially insofar as Pat does reciprocate and does so with quality efforts, this strengthens in Alice (and in Pat) the belief that their love is mutual. This contributes to each party increasingly internalizing the welfare of the other party.

Bob and Alex are also married, but being devotees of orthodox economics, they draft a very detailed prenuptial contract that will govern their marriage. Bob early on does favors for Alex with good quality, but when he asks himself, "Why?," he settles on the explanation that it was a contractual obligation. Increasingly, he does (only) what he believes are his obligations under the contract. And because even a detailed contract will be incomplete and vague as to quality of performance, his attention fixes on his contractual obligations. Alex behaves similarly; a vicious cycle in terms of each party internalizing the welfare of the other party is the unhappy result.

A FORMAL MODEL?

Constructing a formal model of this story is as simple as the story. In each period $t = 0, 1, \ldots, T$, Alice has the opportunity to do a favor for Pat. She must decide whether to do the favor at all and, if she does, with what quality; write q_t for her decision, where $q_t = 0$ means she chooses not to do the favor, $q_t = 1$ means she does it with consummate care, and $q_t \in (1/2, 1)$ is the favor done but with less than consummate care. In the verbal stories, Pat is faced with similar decisions; to avoid any suspicion that this is an orthodox model of trading favors, the model is one-sided: Alice can do favors for Pat, but not vice versa. The direct cost of the favor done with consummate effort at time t is c_t; if Alice chooses to do the favor with care $q_t < 1$, it costs her $c_t q_t^2$. The direct benefit to Pat of the favor at time t is b_t at most; if Alice does the favor with quality q_t, Pat's benefit is $b_t q_t$. The sequence of cost and benefit parameters $\{(c_t, b_t); t = 0, 1, \ldots\}$ is an i.i.d. sequence of random variables; Alice always knows c_t; one can play with variations in the model concerning how much she knows about b_t when deciding whether to do the favor. For simplicity, I'll assume she knows b_t.

At time 0, Alice makes a decision about q_0 balancing her interests and Pat's: She chooses q_0 to maximize

$$k_0 q_0 b_0 - q_0^2 c_0 \quad \text{for } q_t \in \{0\} \cup (1/2, 0),$$

where k_0 is some initial parameter reflecting her love for Pat as a newlywed. And, thereafter, she chooses q_t to maximize $k_t q_t b_t - q_t^2 c_t$, where a "transition function" specifies the evolution of k_t from k_{t-1} and q_{t-1}; say, $k_t = \phi(k_{t-1}, q_{t-1})$, where ϕ is appropriately increasing in q_{t-1}.

I doubt that you need me to explain how one would change the model for Bob and Alex; because they have a contract, the evolution of Bob's $\{k_t\}$ will be governed by a very different transition rule $k_t = \psi(k_{t-1}, q_{t-1})$.

Please note that, as trivial as is this "model," there is still at least one implicit assumption baked into it: Alice is myopic. She doesn't take into account, at time t, how her decision q_t will affect k_{t+1} and subsequent values of k_{t+s}. This, I contend, captures the spirit of Bem's theory.[1]

Indeed, Bem's story is, I'm told by experts, an "as if" story. After Alice does a favor for Pat, it is "as if" she consciously asked herself *Why?* And whatever is the explanation on which she alights, this tendency/attitude is strengthened in her and her future behavior. However, it is not intended or implied that she consciously reasons in this fashion; her behavior (the evolution of her attitudes) is "as if" she did so. Economists can be happy with this, given that "as if" models of behavior in economics are entirely orthodox, even if the notion of preferences evolving is not.

Does this formal "model" add anything to the more verbal story originally told? At this point, the answer is clearly no. One needs to push harder on this model to get something out of it. There should be something that is traded off against leaving it to an individual to "unconsciously determine" his or her evolving attitudes. This late in the book, I'm going to leave this here, but let me reiterate two suggested directions briefly mentioned earlier in the book:

- In the introduction, the possibility of the happily married couple making an informal agreement about who is responsible for which mundane tasks is raised. Such agreements, potentially, lower frictions that may be encountered when, for instance, the bathroom needs cleaning.

Against this is the "warm glow" that might ensue if Alice, unbidden, simply cleans the bathroom.

- And there is a question posed in chapter 3: it is quite heroic to assume that Alice knows what Pat wants; e.g., which favors are most important to Pat. Thinking about how this process is affected by the degree of communication between Pat and Alice about each others' preferences—hence what each party reveals about those preferences—introduces some trade-offs into the story.

CAN EXTRINSIC REWARDS ENHANCE INTRINSIC MOTIVATION, REDUX?

In cases where extrinsic rewards enhance intrinsic motivation—think of stock options for lower-level employees that enhance the sense that the employee is an owner or team member—the self-perception-theory process may strengthen the enhancement. Bob, given stock options, sees himself in the moment as owner and team member of the start-up for which he works. He provides consummate effort in the moment, working long hours and assisting fellow employees when he can, for the greater good. And, in "justifying" his efforts, his self-perceived identity as an owner and team member strengthens in him the perception that this is who he is, leading to even greater efforts going forward.

An interesting question about this arises from research by Roland Fryer and associates. To motivate inner-city students to raise their grades in a randomized controlled trial, Fryer offered to pay students' cell-phone bills if they "succeeded." In one treatment group, success was defined as achieving higher grades. In a second group, "success" was based on the number of books read by the subjects. Fryer found that the incentives did not improve the grades of students in the first treatment group; an explanation is that the students might have been motivated to try to raise their grades, but they didn't know how to do so. Students in the second treatment group, however, did see improvement in their grades (correlated with the number of books they read).[2]

The experiment ends when the payments stop. But, in the current context, the question of interest is, What happens to the number of books read by students when the payments stop, relative to the number of books read before and during the experiment? Will students who had intrinsic motivation to read books before the experiment have lost that intrinsic motivation? (Recall that in the Lepper, Green, and Nisbett experiment with children at Bing Nursery School, kids observed to have high intrinsic motivation for drawing elaborate pictures who were extrinsically rewarded for doing so seemed to lose at least some of that intrinsic motivation when the rewards were withdrawn.[3]) Or will students, having learned the connection between higher grades and book reading (a matter of inference and not preferences) continue to read more books? Or, a third possibility, will students, having been encouraged to read books through extrinsic rewards, having found that doing so is fun, therefore continue to read once the extrinsic rewards are taken away? Data are lacking, so the answers to these questions remain a matter of speculation.

MOTIVATION ON THE JOB?

The importance of this dynamic in economics—if you grant the existence of this dynamic at all—is surely greater if it applies not only to marriage and to other examples of social relationships such as friendship but also to employment relationships as well. And, I contend, it does.

In many employment situations, the connection of the employee to his or her job is instrumental. For such an employee, the best answer to the question, "What connects you to your work?," is "They pay me, I work." But in other cases, the connection is expressive; that is, it is part of the individual's identity. Answers to "What connects you . . . ?" can take a variety of forms:

- "I love what I do, because the work is interesting and exciting to me." Think, for instance, of a bench scientist or engineer engaged in creating an innovative product. Or think of a scholar at a research university who loves the thrill of doing research and the satisfaction that comes from learning something new.
- "I love what I do, because it serves a greater social purpose." Think, for instance, of a doctor working for Médicins Sans Frontières. Or think of a scholar at a research university whose research is aimed at influencing public policy.
- "I love what I do, because of the mission we (at my job) are all on." Think of an engineer working for NASA in the 1960s with the mission of reaching the moon by the end of the decade. Or think of a scholar at a professional

school or a small liberal arts college for whom teaching is personally fulfilling.

- "I love the people with whom I work."
- "I love the organization for which I work."

Expressive connections can, of course, involve more than one of these. My contention is that, for any of these expressive connections that work, self-perception-theory processes can, over time, strengthen those connections. In the previous chapter, I mentioned engineers and scientists pursuing technical perfection at the cost of getting a product ready for market in an organization whose culture celebrates technical achievements; and I mentioned the institution of primary care nursing, in which senior RNs are "rewarded" at least in part by the bonds they form with "their" patients. In both cases, work practices and culture will, over time, strengthen the attitudes of the individual employee, for better in some cases and for worse in others, when it comes to the interests of the employer.[4]

Or, to give a close-to-home caricature, consider three graduate schools of business, A, B, and C. School A has a culture and a reward system—not just financial rewards, but esteem from colleagues and influence over decisions—that rewards excellence in professional education. "Research" is defined to include—indeed, is primarily—the study of so-called best current practice in specific firms and industries, followed by documenting those practices in a form that can be used in the professional-degree classroom.

School C, on the other hand, has a founding charter that states the following:

Systematic research matters; teaching follows. Research [is the] fundamental engine of progress.

Research should be descriptive above all, especially to understand business and organizations; prescription could follow, in practice.

Such research should be rooted in a set of underlying disciplines, notably economics, psychology, and mathematics. These should also be central to master's-level courses, as well as being the foundations of such business functions as finance, marketing, and accounting.

The classroom is a place to ground the students in the skills of analytical problem solving, in the style of operations research, or "management science."

Particular attention should be given to doctoral studies, to stimulate research and have the graduates carry these ideas to other schools.

Faculty members at school C are rewarded, both tangibly and in terms of praise, prestige, and influence, on the basis of their publications in journals such as *Econometrica* and the *Journal of Personality and Social Psychology*.

And school B takes a middle ground, insisting that school-C-style research should be on equal footing with professional-program education; school B's motto is *Balanced Excellence*.[5]

Take a freshly minted PhD student from a leading department of economics and plop her down in one of these three institutions as first employer. Because I've seen it in action, I am confident in predicting: either the young scholar will quickly find another employer or she will come to embrace the cultural values of the employer. Of course, this involves the individual's nature. But the power of social identity theory—individuals take on the beliefs, attitudes, and emotions that distinguish a valued group to which they (aspire) to belong and which distinguish this group from "out-groups" to which they don't belong—together with self-perception-theory forces will nurture in the young scholar attitudes that reflect those of her institution, as well as attitudes that her institution has it "right."[6]

I can offer firsthand testimony as someone who grew up in what is (essentially) school B: the school-B model is best, both in terms of the quality of research its faculty members produce and the professional education it offers. I know some young scholars whose first job was at a school-A-model school and other young scholars whose first job was at a school-C-model school, all of whom took on the values of their institution, all of whom mistakenly believe that their school's model is best.

This is, of course, anecdotal. Running a randomized controlled experimental test of this hypothesis is probably impossible. And, perhaps, it only applies to unworldly academic types. However, if anyone should be able to resist these sorts of social psychological pressures, it ought to be young economists, whose training equips them with a firm belief in *de gustibus* and cynicism concerning the other social sciences. Keynes famously wrote that "practical men who believe themselves to be quite exempt from any intellectual influence, are usually the slaves of some defunct economist." Turning this somewhat on its head, I contend that young economists, who believe themselves to be secure in their

God-or-genetically-given own tastes and attitudes, are usually the slaves of some defunct social psychologist.

The bottom line is that institutions of all sorts—public and private, for-profit and not-for-profit—can and do use these social psychological processes as tools to shape the attitudes of their employees, for better or for worse in terms of the activities of those employees. If one aspires to understand human resource management, understanding these processes is important. And, while these processes have attracted some attention among economists, they deserve a lot more.

13

SHOULD ECONOMISTS MOVE IN THESE DIRECTIONS?

It will not have escaped the reader's attention that this book consists primarily of stories that are prefaced with words such as *if* and *suppose*. And, in the few simple formal models presented, I can fairly be accused of arriving at conclusions that are no more than a few simple steps from the assumptions. This raises two obvious questions:

- Should economists engage in models of this sort or should they adhere to the well-established principle of *de gustibus*, leaving preference formation for psychologists, sociologists, and other social scientists?
- Do we learn anything from the sort of models I've presented? Will models that incorporate context and experience-driven preferences lead to insights beyond obvious conclusions derived directly from questionable assumptions?

Concerning the second question, I propose two answers. First, if there is good evidence that individual behavior, especially individual dynamic behavior, varies systematically from orthodox economic models—and, of course, I believe there is good evidence of this—then conclusions drawn from models that are built out of better models of behavior are worthwhile, even if they lack any subtlety. And second, the proof of the pudding is in the eating. We won't know whether significant new insights will emerge until we try. Perhaps this will lead nowhere. But going down blind alleys to no useful result is nothing new to economics, and the potential prize justifies the effort.

Both these answers suppose that the answer to the first question is yes; that this is a direction that economists ought to pursue. And there is a solid argument to be made that the answer to the first question is no.

Economics as a way of thinking and analyzing various categories of social exchange has and continues to generate many valuable insights into important issues. It derives its strength from its disciplined way of thinking, a way of thinking that is based on Solow's three canonical principles, greed, rationality, and equilibrium.[1] Each of these three limits the questions that economic thinking can address, but they strengthen what can be said in contexts better suited to economic reasoning.

Psychology as a discipline involves a different way of organizing thought and analysis. (Sociology and political sciences are still others.) I like to quote my colleague Dale Miller on the fundamental difference in how economists and psychologists approach things: "Economists like to show how seemingly different things are actually the same. Psychologists like to show how seemingly similar things are actually different."

Granting that this description of the two disciplines is accurate, it would seem that the two are fundamentally incompatible.

Hence: Economists should "stay in their lane," leaving questions that their methodology is ill suited to tackle to other disciplines, so as not to weaken the power of that methodology when it comes to questions for which economic thinking is well suited.

Perhaps, Gary Becker notwithstanding, economists should recognize that the methods of economics are ill suited to prescribing how to manage marital relations, leaving this for psychologists. To offer a more controversial example, despite heroic efforts by many eminent economists, I believe that, at this point, psychology tells us much more about bilateral bargaining than does economics.[2]

My problem with this argument for retaining *de gustibus* is: What are we to do with subjects that blend significant economics and other social sciences? This includes, for instance, the topics discussed in Akerlof and Kranton and in Bowles.[3] My own interests are, as noted throughout this book, in human resource management (HRM). HRM is certainly a topic of importance in economics: labor exchange is central to market exchange, and I contend that one can't understand labor markets in the aggregate without understanding microfounded labor exchange, which is HRM or what Lazear has termed "personnel economics."[4] I contend further that employment relationships are both economic and social in character.[5] While one can gain much insight into HRM from a purely orthodox-economics perspective (as in Lazear and Gibbs[6]), those insights must be tempered with insights from the other social sciences, most notably social psychology, to get the full picture.

The choice, then, is whether (1) to put forward insights from the two separate disciplinary perspectives, leaving the blending of those insights to the informed intuition of practitioners, or (2) to incorporate enough flexibility in one or the other discipline to deal more completely with the full range of issues that arise.

When it comes to abandoning *de gustibus* (or not), I think—and I hope I've convinced you—that economists can fruitfully formulate and analyze models in which preferences (a better term would be the *objective* the individual seeks to attain in the moment) are formed on the basis of the context in which choices are being made and evolve on the basis of the individual's experiences. And, for my colleagues who object that this loosens the discipline imposed by *de gustibus* so much so that all discipline is lost, I offer a bit of the recent history of economic thought in response.

When noncooperative game theory, allied with information economics, became fashionable in the field of industrial organization (IO), "orthodox" IO expert Franklin Fisher mounted a spirited attack against these practices. In "Games Economists Play: A Noncooperative View," Fisher decries this (at the time, new) fashion as at best a waste of time and, perhaps worse, a waste of the valuable talent of otherwise capable young scholars who were being led astray.[7] Fisher's primary objection is an objection that can be applied to the simple models of this book: the conclusions were a product, and a not very subtle or complex product, of assumptions made by the modeler. The term "backward engineering" can be applied, although I don't think Fisher is impolite enough to use that term. Instead, Fisher distinguishes between *generalizing theory*—general equilibrium and the welfare theorems are his example—in which broadly valid conclusions follow from very general assumptions, and *exemplifying theory*, which shows things that might be true, if you agree with the very specific assumptions being made. The game-theoretic "advances" in IO were all exemplifying theory, proving nothing and therefore, according to Fisher, teaching us nothing.

I have a lot of sympathy for Fisher's argument. To be exact, I have a lot of sympathy for the second part of his argument; I don't see the assumptions of general equilibrium as being all that general. General equilibrium theory and the first theorem of welfare economics don't teach us that markets are efficient; rather, they teach us how many special assumptions are required to conclude that market are efficient and in how many ways inefficiencies appear.[8] If there are any good examples of generalizing theory in economics—perhaps *prices settle in commodity markets to equate supply and demand, at least in the short run and only as an approximation*—then they are few and far between.

But, if I may paraphrase Fisher's argument, proving a proposition about a game-theoretic model in IO or in any other field in economics does not equal establishing a fact about the real world. Any number of formal models in economics begin with silly assumptions and derive conclusions that may be subtle but which are just silly. It takes empiricism—casual empiricism (common sense, in other words) at a minimum; and preferably serious laboratory or field-based empiricism—to "establish" facts about the real world. Theory has a crucial role here; it gives structure to empirical efforts. But theory is just the beginning of the process. And Fisher, at the time, was observing a lot of beginnings with few middles or ends.[9]

So, to conclude: while *de gustibus* makes for strong discipline and, hence, a strong discipline, it makes for pretty limited and even misleading social science in contexts that are central to economics. Individuals making economic decisions are indeed influenced by the specific context in which the decisions are taken and by the history that precedes the current moment. Economists should embrace this—I'll use the word "fact"—and with care, circumspection, and empirical testing, carefully run with it.

COMMENTARY

Joseph E. Stiglitz

It's a real pleasure to be able to comment on David's Arrow Lecture for multiple reasons.

This is the thirteenth Arrow Lecture, a long line of distinguished lectures following up, in one way or another, on Ken's multiple seminal contributions. Arrow was Columbia's most distinguished PhD in economics. I hold him and his thesis up to our PhD students for what we expect for all of our PhDs. Not all of them have achieved that, I have to say.

This lecture has particular meaning for me because Ken was my teacher in the fall of 1964, a few years ago, at MIT, and over the subsequent decades, Ken Arrow and I became colleagues and good friends—on one occasion he even entrusted me with babysitting his goldfish. He was an intellectual mentor for me, as he was for the entire profession. He changed the way we think and the way we do economics. He changed our preferences, in many ways, about what we think about—about what is "good economics." For years, Ken would come back to his alma mater for this lecture, sitting in the front row, often joined by his sons, David and Andy, and sometimes by his wife, Selma. He always had a yellow notepad in hand, and the first and most insightful comment after the lecture would come from Ken himself. And he continued to stun us with his brilliance, as he had at the IMSSS workshops to which David refers. It was, of course, all a little bit intimidating for young economists.

When I began my work in economics, it seemed that many of both the central conclusions and assumptions were suspect, including the conclusions concerning the efficiency of the market economy. The question I and my classmates, most importantly George Akerlof, asked each other, was how to begin a reformulation in a conservative profession, wedded to its assumptions and very slow to change. The assumptions in the first fundamental welfare theorem of fixed and exogenous preferences and technologies, fixed beliefs and perfect, or at least exogenous information, with no private information, all seemed crucial. While the assumption of fixed preferences was obviously—to me, at least—the most glaring deficiency, it was the hardest to fix. Becker and Stigler and others made it clear that any attempt to do so would encounter enormous resistance. They wrote a paper entitled De Gustibus Non Est Disputandum, "tastes are not to be disputed." And it seemed obvious that information was imperfect and exogenous, and that there were already insights from statistics that would help us develop mathematical formalizations that would make the new ideas more acceptable. I should add that even then we encountered enormous resistance from the leading journals. George Akerlof—it's not giving away secrets—has written that his famous lemons paper was rejected three times before it was finally accepted at the *QJE* (which should give a little bit of encouragement to those of you who write papers and find them rejected; rejection is not a sign that it's going to be a pathbreaking paper, but it's not inconsistent with it being a pathbreaking paper).[1]

One of the things about Ken that was most impressive was that not only had he established the sense in which and the conditions under which Adam Smith's invisible hand conjecture was correct, but also he went on to think more deeply about the real-world implications. Contrary to Chicago School economists who thought he and Debreu had established the efficiency of the market, he realized he had really proved that markets were not, in general, efficient. And this goes back to the foundations of economics—when we prove a theorem, it's just a theorem: the question is, what is the connection between the theorem and the world. And people reading the first fundamental theorem in Chicago for some reason came to the conclusion it proved that the markets were efficient. And when I read it, I thought it proved that markets were not efficient because the conditions were almost surely never satisfied. What was distinctive about Ken was that he was not satisfied with proving these results, which came to be called the *fundamental theorems of welfare economics*; he went on to explore ideas such as moral hazard and adverse selection, endogenous technology, and even endogenous preferences and institutional responses to market failures that went well beyond the standard competitive model (I'll say a little bit about those later), and how they might affect the efficiency of the economy. Over time, it also became increasingly clear that the sufficient conditions for efficiency that he had established were close to necessary conditions.

While the big breakthrough in the 1970s and 1980s of behavioral economics undermined assumptions of full rationality, those developments were based on the recognition of cognitive limitations—thinking fast versus thinking slow—and brought insights from psychology into economics. By contrast, the lecture here, and work by a number of other scholars in the past two decades, focuses on preference formation and is influenced more by sociology and social psychologists, including some of those cited by Kreps. It's not a matter of thinking fast or slow. The problems David talks about—marriage, giving blood, giving a lecture—are not the result of fast thinking. The parties to these discussions deliberate slowly: You don't solve those problems that David solved, those game theory problems that he solved, in just a second; it takes a few more seconds than that. And so they deliberate slowly, aware that behavior is more complex, and different, from that hypothesized in the standard economists' model and in ways that matter deeply, at least for key relationships, not just marriage, but in labor and credit markets. David talked about labor markets; I'll give an example a little bit later related to credit markets.

The Harvard philosopher Michael Sandel, in his very entertaining book *What Money Can't Buy: The Moral Limits of Markets*, provides many examples, besides those provided by David, where what might be termed marketization changes the nature of the economic exchange and relationship, where market norms can crowd out valuable nonmarket behavior—with extrinsic rewards crowding out intrinsic.[2]

I think that's really an important idea and needs to be modeled, and I think what David here has done is an important beginning. I am not sure that the literature provides an adequate taxonomy of the various channels through which the effects are exercised and the ways in which this kind of analysis is differentiated from the individualistic analysis that has been at the center of economics. But the careful reasoning provided by Kreps is an important step forward, helping us to think more rigorously how we can best integrate other-regarding behavior in individuals' decision making.

Along the way, what David says has much to say about currently fashionable traditions in, say, macroeconomics—although he may not have explicitly said that. As I have also emphasized, there is a marked difference between choices between red and green lettuce—choices that we make repeatedly, and, on the basis of which, using the theory of revealed preferences, we can construct a preference ordering, a utility function—and lifetime choices: we live only once, we don't know how we will feel in the future. Unless we believe in reincarnation, we can't rerun the experiment. Individuals can reason, "I wished I had saved more or less, and my lifetime utility would accordingly have been larger or smaller." The economists' model is deficient not only in its assumption of fixed preferences but also in its assumptions that we know what will make us happy or well off.

The key aspect emphasized and modeled by David is that intrinsic rewards of other-regarding behavior may be attenuated by contractual terms. He uses this as at least a partial explanation of why we don't see punishments in certain contexts where, in the standard framework, they would be required to achieve efficient outcomes. He emphasizes that the utility an individual gets—and his or her behavior—is affected by the contractual relationship in which the individual is embedded. That is very much in the spirit of Karl Polanyi, who argued in his seminal book *The Great Transformation* that markets are embedded in politics and society, and the design of market arrangements has to reflect that.[3] I'll say a little bit more about that later.

In the remaining time, I want to turn to three central issues posed by the endogeneity and interdependence of preferences and behavior.

The first concerns alternative conceptions of preferences. Adam Smith, of course, in his *Theory of Moral Sentiments*, recognized the other-regarding nature of human beings and the importance of it for behavior.[4] It has taken a long time for economists to begin to formalize what this implies, and Kreps's lecture will be, I believe, a fundamental contribution to this literature.

But Kreps also begins an enquiry into *changes* in preferences. That preferences are changing, and can be changed, at least to some extent, is obvious: parents spend enormous efforts trying to "shape" their children. Those in marketing and corporations believe that the billions of dollars they spend affects consumer behavior. Those in HR in corporations believe that team building and corporate culture can affect behavior—every bit as much, or more, than monetary incentives, and in many ways more efficiently. The idea was to get workers' utility functions aligned with the interests of the firms so that they do what the firms want them to do in circumstances as they evolve. This is an alternative resolution posed by the necessity of delegation. The principal (the owner of the firm) can't do everything, and the question the literature until now has focused on is how can the principal give incentives for them to do what he or she wants. The alternative that has begun to be discussed, for instance by Akerlof and Kranton, is to get their preferences aligned, to get their identity aligned.[5]

There is a long literature on changing preferences, including habit formation. There are difficult issues about commitment and foresight: to what extent can individuals, knowing that their preferences tomorrow will be different, commit themselves to behave according to their current preferences? How do and should—though I'm not sure I know what the word "should" means here—individuals behave?

There is one strand of work in which individuals have a meta utility function and choose a utility function next period to maximize the meta utility function. That approach is comfortable for economists because it's all about choosing something to maximize something else—that's what we do all the time—but I think misses a key aspect of endogenous preferences: the extent to which what we experience and how we respond to those experiences is at least partly out of our control.

I am attracted more to an approach more common in psychology, where there are multiple identities, preferences, and that which is "expressed" is largely determined by context. The banker who acts less selfishly after going to church on Sunday than he does during the week is not doing so consciously, but as a result of the context in which he is in. He has been moved out of a world in which the money metric dominates into a world in which social welfare dominates. He, of course, has put himself into that context, but I am unconvinced that as he alternates between these different "selves" he is doing so in ways that could convincingly be shown to reflect some underlying metapreference. That this is so is a strong assumption, yet to be tested.

There is an alternative way of putting some of this, perhaps more in the standard formulation of behavioral economics: Individuals have preferences over *framed* options. The frame depends not just on context (for instance, the penalty option that Kreps would have if he were a no-show). The lens through which we see the world is crucial, and those lenses are largely culturally determined. Perception—how we see the world—is a construction; the categories, prototypes, images, narratives, and other mental structures that a person has in his mind mediate his perceptions and affect what he believes, and therefore how he behaves.

Now I want to discuss the determinants of preferences. A central tenet of more recent work on endogenous preferences is that those preferences are affected by the behavior of others, as well as by history and culture. We don't choose where we are born and where we grow up, central determinants of our behavior. Our preferences, in that sense, are interdependent. But while we are affected by "society" at large, we are, collectively, society at large.

There is an evolutionary process at play and in simple models, we can even describe a Nash equilibrium. David asked, "What can economists bring to this?," Sociologists don't think in terms of a social equilibrium, but thinking this way is part of the DNA of economists—looking at interactions and how A affects B, and B affects C, and C affects A. Economists' mind-set and toolkit means that there is a real potential for us to make a contribution in this area.

Finally, let me come to the question of the importance of these effects, and the big question that David asked: Should we model this? From my perspective, the answer is unambiguously yes. If preferences are endogenous, and if we can systematically understand the dynamics of preference change, then it offers a new set of tools—a new set of insights into why certain policies have failed, and it gives us potentially a new set of tools for bringing about social change.

One of the reasons I got into this area of endogenous preference is because of my interests in development economics. Development is about modernization, and modernization is about changing preferences. Weber, for instance, wrote about the central role of the Protestant ethic in the development of capitalism.[6] The World Bank's 2015 World Development Report, called *Mind, Society and Behavior*, provided glimpses into the beginning of a development agenda centered around changing beliefs and preferences.[7]

Let me illustrate by considering a key developmental innovation in the latter part of the 20th century, related to capital markets: microcredit. There were numerous RCTs (randomized controlled trials) trying to "perfect" the microcredit loan contract, asking "how do we tweak the contract to make the best loan contract possible?" They did a lot of experiments to try to get better contracts, along the lines of Becker's idea that every marriage needs a prenuptial contract. But then came the enormous failure of the largest microcredit scheme, in India, SK—some of you may know about that. To many of us, including to Muhammad Yunus (the founder of the first microcredit scheme, the Grameen bank, and who was awarded the Nobel Peace Prize for his work), with whom I had an opportunity to talk about this failure, it did not come as a surprise. SK was a for-profit lender, and having a for-profit lender totally changed the relationship between the lender and the borrower. And so this is a case in which it was the perception about who was on the other side of the contract, and what was his relationship with me, what he was doing for or to me, that mattered. The critical difference between SK and Grameen, accounting for the failure of one and the success of the other, was that Grameen Bank was a non-profit, and SK, the Indian company, was a for-profit lender. And that totally changed the dynamic between the borrower and the lender. It changed the "intrinsic reward" associated with repaying the loan.

So the unambiguous answer, for me, to the question David asked us, should we model this, is yes. There is a growing body of literature on how history, culture, and those around us shape preferences. I made an attempt to model historical and cultural effects on behavior in a paper with Karla Hoff in 2016.[8] I think this is a key frontier of economics because it helps explain social change, diverging paths of development, and societal rigidities.

Ken would have given a similar answer. Indeed, as we look at and think about Ken's work, we do a little Google search, only to discover the existence of articles that have not entered into the main economic agenda. He wrote an article in 2010 on "The Economy of Trust," and he gave a seminar at the World Bank on that subject 10 years earlier, which he published in a journal called *Religion and Liberty*. (Those of you who knew Ken knew that he had interest in everything and was really involved in everything.) In that article he wrote, "I believe that sociology should play more of a role in economics than it does. The way people behave in economics is partly influenced by how other people behave." So it is really this broader range of interactions among people, going well beyond that captured in the standard model of individuals with fixed preferences trading in markets, that he called attention to. There is, of course, much more to be said on each of these topics. Ken would have been enormously pleased with this lecture, he would have had much to say. I can only thank David once again for this thoughtful and stimulating lecture.

COMMENTARY

Alessandra Casella

I would like to offer two short comments. The two comments are related and in fact also related to points that have been raised in the previous observations

First of all, we should note that David Kreps focuses on *individual choices*, and yet, we can easily extend his message to *social choice*, very much in the spirit of Ken Arrow. There is a literature, again at the boundary with social psychology, that makes the following claim: *Keeping constant policies and payoffs, decisions reached democratically have higher legitimacy, and hence compliance.*

It is not difficult to find examples that are in line with the claim. A traditional reference in this context comes from Switzerland: Swiss cantons with more referenda have lower tax evasion. A second example comes from industrial organization: firms with more workers' involvement tend to have higher productivity.

Even if we accept the observations as facts, as proof of the claim these examples have a problem: the samples can suffer from self-selection. It is perfectly possible, even likely, that more civic-minded cantons have both higher reliance on direct democracy—more and better attended referenda—and lower tax evasion. Similarly, it seems quite plausible that firms with a more productive workforce also have workers who want to be more involved in decision making.

Testing the claim then requires keeping the samples constant while modifying the institutions only: for given civic-mindedness, does compliance increase if a tax has been decided by referendum rather than by a legislature? For given samples of workers, does productivity increase if workers are given more say in decision making? The problem is that in historical data, the samples are hardly constant. What is needed then are experimental tests.

Two excellent examples are two papers by Pedro Dal Bo' and Andrew Foster with other coauthors.[1] The idea is simple (and here I paraphrase the 2019 working paper): participants engage in some task (adding numbers); they may be compensated by a fixed salary or be paid piece-rate, and in this latter case, their earnings will depend on the number of correct tasks they accomplish. The compensation method can either be assigned randomly by a computer or decided by the group via majority voting. Conditional on being paid piece-rate, is productivity higher when the compensation scheme was chosen by the group?

I am sorry to report that the answer is in fact negative—Dal Bo' and co-authors do not find any productivity difference in this experiment. On the other hand, they do find an effect in the 2010 article, although the experiment there is more complex, and confounding factors could be playing a role. A fair conclusion then is that we do not know. It remains a very interesting question.

The second point I would like to raise is related, because again it is linked to the *social* rather than individual reading of context. Here my claim is the following: *How context is read depends on social norms, and social norms are sticky but not immutable.*

Contrary to David Kreps, I am not ready to discard Becker's point about premarital contracts: if detailed contracts became the norm, their meaning as signal, including self-signals, would likely disappear.

Let me propose a second example. I will mimic Professor Kreps's rhetorical device and use real names and imaginary episodes.

Suppose that here at Columbia we are working to organize the Arrow Lecture. Delighted as we are at its prospect, two weeks before the lecture we realize we have a problem: there is not a single woman on the podium.

Thus, we decide to ask Alessandra Casella (AC) to participate. And AC is happy to do so, because the lecture is in honor of Ken Arrow and because the speaker is excellent, the topic very interesting, and the panel impressive.

And yet the situation is complicated. The late invitation and its wording make focal one identity (woman) that is not the identity that should be relevant in this setting (scholar). As we learn from David Kreps, this may also negatively affect AC's future self-image.

But there are other aspects to the question. It is important for young women and men to become used to seeing women on the podium, even in economics. And the more that happens, the more the norm shifts, until the clash between the two identities eventually disappears. From the point of view of AC then, it is worth facing a little bit of discomfort if it helps to change old norms.

Bringing the message back to identity, identity is socially constructed, and this applies particularly to which aspects of our complex identities become salient in a given context.

Thank you very much, and thank you in particular to David Kreps for a very engaging and stimulating book.

RESPONSE TO THE COMMENTS OF PROFESSORS STIGLITZ AND CASELLA

I'm grateful to Professors Casella and Stiglitz for their generous comments. I find myself in agreement with nearly everything they say, but there are a few specific comments I can offer in response.

Professor Stiglitz's comments range over a number of topics and, as I read them, I find myself thinking not "yes, but," but instead "yes, and in addition . . ." Here are two of my "in additions."

Early in his comments, he describes the ideas promoted here as different from work in behavioral economics that focuses on cognitive limitations and biases; he cites Kahnemann's "thinking fast and slow," but one could also cite Thaler and Sunstein's theory of "nudges," as well as many other cognitive biases.[1] This is indeed another aspect of behavior that economists should make part of the mainstream. And a third aspect is the use of heuristics at various levels of complexity; from the work of Gigerenzer to, for instance, Sargent's models of the consequences of learning from misspecified OLS regressions.[2] Consider in this regard

Solow's canonical principles of greed, rationality, and equilibrium.[3] The present book seeks to loosen the strict bonds of greed. The four books cited in this paragraph go after rationality. One expects (hopes?) that equilibrium will similarly be up for debate.[4]

Professor Stiglitz also mentions, almost in passing, the idea that individuals learn their "preferences" from experiences they have. Knowing that this can happen leads to a primitive desire to experiment with new things, to learn and grow. In chapter 3, I briefly described surveys on motivation I have run on various groups of executives at the Stanford GSB for executive education. In another part of the survey instrument, and following the work of Heath, I ask respondents to say how powerful a motivator for them are things such as pay, praise, and job security, but also things such as "learning and growing" and "feeling good about what they do."[5] In all surveys that I can recall, "learning and growing" gets the highest average score, significantly higher than the average scores for pay, praise, and job security. Of course, there is some sample selection bias at work; these are folks who have chosen to attend an executive education program. But one can wonder: What are the economic consequences of curiosity as a fundamental driver of behavior? What does this do to economic notions of efficiency?

Turning to the comments of Professor Casella, she cites the experimental work of Foster, Dal Bo', and Putterman and of Dal Bo', Foster, and Kamei concerning the proposition that *keeping constant policies and payoffs, decisions reached democratically have higher legitimacy and hence compliance.*[6] One wonders whether "decisions reached democratically" is too broad a category. Amend the condition to "decisions reached with a strong consensus after free debate," and I have a lot more confidence in the consequent assertion. But, and with reference to the current poisonous political climate in the United States, legislative decisions reached on a party-line vote, with limited debate and opportunity to amend, in a very closely divided legislative body, may well excite greater feelings of illegitimacy in the minds of the losing side. One queues here the debate whether direct democracy or constitutional forms that protect the rights of minorities are better, as well as the background (lack of) legitimacy of whatever political system is in place. The devil is in the details.

And she writes, "Contrary to David Kreps, I am not ready to discard Becker's point about premarital contracts: if detailed contracts became the norm, their meaning as signal, including self-signals, would likely disappear."

Of course, this is so. However:

- Becker's claim is that making marital contracts mandatory—that is, a matter of law—would necessarily remove the signaling problem. My point—which I stick to on the basis of the theory of signaling and the inferences drawn from off-path or out-of-equilibrium signals—is that "necessarily" is too strong. Perhaps an equilibrium that Becker would prefer will emerge. Perhaps not. In theory, both are possibilities, and Becker is too quick to dismiss the "bad-equilibrium" possibility.
- And Becker is talking about a legal requirement, while Professor Casella refers to a social norm. These are different things. This is not to say that a legal requirement

wouldn't lead to a positive social norm. It might. But I refer the reader to Bowles's *The Moral Economy* once again, with the speculation—not a prediction, but a possibility—that making prenups a legal requirement will make it harder for a positive social norm to emerge.[7]

APPENDIX

Axiomatic Derivation of the Utility Model of Chapter 3

The primitives are a finite collection of individuals $i = 1, \ldots, I$, with $i = 1$ the distinguished individual, and a finite collection of feasible social states X.

Let P be the space of all probability distributions over X, and let $\mathcal{P} := P^I$. The interpretation of a $\pi = (p_1, \ldots, p_I) \in \mathcal{P}$ is that it is the imaginary situation in which individual i finds himself in social state x with probability $p_i(x)$.

And we suppose that the distinguished individual $i = 1$—call her Alice—has complete and transitive preferences on the space $\mathcal{P}$.

Note that, in the fashion of the Anscombe-Aumann technique, we do not specify the joint distribution with which, say, 1 finds herself in social state x and i finds himself in social state y. By assuming that Alice's preferences over full joint probability distributions over X^I can be represented by her preferences $\succeq$ over $\mathcal{P}$, we are assuming that correlations across individuals in terms of the social states in which they find themselves do not matter to Alice. All that matters to her is the vector of marginal probabilities for each $i \in I$.[1]

In addition to assuming that Alice's preferences $\succeq$ are complete and transitive, assume that they satisfy the mixture-space axioms of Herstein and Milnor.[2] These axioms are based on considering $\mathcal{P}$ as a mixture space, a space in which, for any π and π' from $\mathcal{P}$, and for any $\alpha \in [0,1]$, $\alpha\pi + (1-\alpha)\pi'$ is that element of $\mathcal{P}$ in which, if $\pi = (p_1, \ldots, p_I)$ and $\pi' = (p_1', \ldots, p_I')$, then

$$\alpha\pi + (1-\alpha)\pi' := \left(\alpha p_1 + (1-\alpha)p_1', \ldots, \alpha p_I + (1-\alpha)p_I'\right).$$

With this definition, the mixture-space axioms are:

- *For all π, π', $\hat{\pi}$, and $\hat{\pi}'$ from $\mathcal{P}$ and for all $\alpha \in [0, 1]$, $\alpha\pi + (1-\alpha)\hat{\pi} \succ \alpha\pi' + (1-\alpha)\hat{\pi}$ if and only if $\alpha\pi + (1-\alpha)\hat{\pi}' \succ \alpha\pi' + (1-\alpha)\hat{\pi}'$.*
- *If $\pi > \pi'$, then for any third π'', there exists $\alpha^* \in (0, 1)$ such that $\alpha\pi + (1-\alpha)\pi'' \succ \pi'$ and $\pi \succ \alpha\pi' + (1-\alpha)\pi''$ for all $\alpha \in (\alpha^*, 1]$.*

The first axiom is, more or less, the independence axiom of von Neumann and Morgenstern, and the second axiom is the Archimedean axiom, for those who know these terms.

The following proposition follows immediately from the mixture-space theorem (combined with the finiteness of X and I).

Proposition.[3] *If $\succeq$ is complete and transitive and (for $\succ$ the usual strict preference relation defined from $\succeq$) satisfies the two mixture-space axioms, then there exist functions u_i: $X \to R$, $i = 1, \ldots, I$, such that*

$$\pi = (p_1, \ldots, p_I) \succ \pi' = (p'_1, \ldots, p'_I) \textit{ if and only if}$$
$$\sum_i \sum_x p_i(x) u_i(x) \geq \sum_i \sum_x p'_i(x) u_i(x).$$

Note that if $\pi = (p_1, \ldots, p_I)$ is degenerate for each i—that is, for each i, $p_i(x_i) = 1$ for some $x_i \in X$—then the representing overall utility function for Alice takes the form

$$\sum_i u_i(x_i),$$

which is the form discussed in chapter 3.

Now suppose that some other $\hat{i} \neq 1$, call him Bob, satisfies the same axioms, so that (using superscripts) Bob's preferences are represented by some U^{Bob} taking the form

$$\sum_i u_i^{\text{Bob}}(x_i).$$

And suppose that, fixing all x_i except for $\hat{i}$, Alice's preferences over lotteries on π taking the form

$$\left(x_1, \ldots, x_{\hat{i}-1}, x_{\hat{i}+1}, \ldots, x_I\right)$$

coincide with Bob's. Then by standard uniqueness results arising from the mixture-space theorem,

$$u_{\text{Bob}}^{\text{Alice}} \equiv k_{\text{Alice,Bob}}\, u_{\text{Bob}}^{\text{Bob}},$$

where $k_{\text{Alice,Bob}} > 0$. (Obvious variations on this assumption give us the cases where $k_{\text{Alice,Bob}} = 0$ and $k_{\text{Alice,Bob}} < 0$.)[4]

NOTES

PREFACE: KENNETH ARROW AND THIS BOOK

1. Kenneth J. Arrow, "Gifts and Exchanges," *Philosophy and Public Affairs* 1 (1972): 343–62.
2. In the interests of full disclosure, I must add that in this paper Arrow is skeptical of the empirical relevance of some things for which I advocate.
3. Some of those drafts were coauthored with Bengt Holmstrom, who shares in any credit and escapes any blame for what is here.
4. James N. Baron and David M. Kreps, *Strategic Human Resources; Frameworks for General Managers* (New York: Wiley, 1999); David M. Kreps, *The Motivation Toolkit* (New York: Norton, 2018).

INTRODUCTION: GARY BECKER ON PRENUPS

1. The column is available from the *Hoover Digest* (1998) under the title "Do You Swear to Love, Honor, and Cherish? Then Sign Here." Becker's views on the stability of preferences are more nuanced than this introduction suggests. I'll discuss those views in chapter 4; for the time being, I admit to picking on a great economist somewhat unfairly.

2. Oliver E. Williamson, *The Economic Institutions of Capitalism* (New York: Free Press, 1987).
3. A famous article by Stigler and Becker bears the title "De Gustibus Non Est Disputandum"; see George Stigler and Gary Becker, "De Gustibus non est Disputandum," *American Economic Review* 67 (1977): 76–90. To be clear, my argument is with the broader principle—what Stigler and Becker label the "traditional view"—that economists should leave the explanation of tastes to other social scientists and the (often implicit) further assumption that tastes or preferences are fixed, unchanging. See the discussion of Becker's further writing on this topic in chapter 4
4. Darryl J. Bem, "Self-Perception: An Alternative Interpretation of Cognitive Dissonance Phenomena," *Psychology Review* 74, no. 3 (1967): 183–200
5. Michael Sandel, *What Money Can't Buy: The Moral Limits of Markets* (New York: Farrar, Straus and Giroux, 2013).
6. Henry J. Aaron, abstract of "Distinguished Lecture on Economics in Government: Public Policy, Values, and Consciousness," *Journal of Economic Perspectives* 8 (1994): 3–21. Abstract available at https://www.aeaweb.org/articles?id=10.1257/jep.8.2.3.
7. See, for example, Herbert Gintis, "A Radical Analysis of Welfare Economics and Individual Development," *Quarterly Journal of Economics* 86 (1972): 572–99; George A. Akerlof and Janet Yellen, "Gang Behavior, Law Enforcement, and Community Values," in *Value and Public Policy*, ed. Henry J. Aaron, Thomas E. Mann, and Timothy Taylor (Washington, DC: Brookings Institution, 1993), 173–209; George A. Akerlof and Rachel E. Kranton, *Identity Economics* (Princeton, NJ: Princeton University Press, 2010); Samuel Bowles and Herbert Gintis, *A Cooperative Species: Human Reciprocity and Its Evolution* (Princeton, NJ: Princeton University Press, 2011); Samuel Bowles and Sandra Polanía-Reyes, "Economic Incentives and Social Preferences: Substitutes or Complements?," *Journal of Economic Literature*

50 (2012): 368–425; Samuel Bowles, *The Moral Economy: Why Good Incentives Are No Substitute for Good Citizens* (New Haven, CT: Yale University Press, 2016).

8. James N. Baron and David M. Kreps, *Strategic Human Resources; Frameworks for General Managers* (New York: John Wiley & Sons, 1999); David M. Kreps, *The Motivation Toolkit* (New York: Norton, 2018).
9. Richard M. Titmuss, *The Gift Relationship: From Human Blood to Social Policy* (1970), reissue, ed. Ann Oakley and John Aston (New York: New Press, 1997); Roland Bénabou and Jean Tirole, "Incentives and Prosocial Behavior," *American Economic Review* 96 (2006): 1652–78.
10. In my models, the principal may pay for good performance, or the agent may pay a penalty for bad performance, or both.

1. *DE GUSTIBUS NON EST DISPUTANDUM:* THE MAINSTREAM ECONOMIC ACCOUNT OF INDIVIDUAL BEHAVIOR

1. Indeed, many economists adhere to the so-called common-prior or Harsanyi doctrine, which holds that prior assessments by different individuals must agree, leading to the conclusion that two HEs cannot agree to disagree over their posterior assessments if those posterior assessments are common knowledge between them. This doctrine is not universally accepted, and those who disagree with it do not completely disqualify themselves from orthodoxy, even if their work is treated with suspicion.

2. INTRINSIC MOTIVATION

1. Ernst Fehr and Armin Falk, "Psychological Foundations of Incentives," *European Economic Review* 46, no. 4–5 (2002): 687–724.
2. See, for instance, David M. Kreps, *Microeconomic Foundations II: Imperfect Competition, Information, and Strategic Interaction*

(Princeton, NJ: Princeton University Press, 2023), chap. 22, and the model known as *exchanging favors*.

3. In an essay titled "How Did Economics Get That Way and What Way Did It Get" prepared for a conference of the American Academy of Arts and Sciences and subsequently published in *Daedalus* (1997), Robert Solow identifies the three canonical principles of economics as equilibrium, rationality, and greed. While greed is, in fact, commonplace in economic models, *clear purpose* is probably a better canonical term.

3. INTERNALIZING THE WELFARE OF SPECIFIC OTHERS

1. Kenneth J. Arrow, "Gifts and Exchanges," *Philosophy and Public Affairs* 1 (1972): 343–62.
2. "In some circumstances" takes us into the realm of identity economics, which is discussed in chapter 4.
3. Interested readers can see a full account of these survey results in David M. Kreps, *The Motivation Toolkit* (New York: Norton, 2018), including cross-tabs against demographic characteristics of the respondents. Three points about the full survey results are worth mentioning here:

    - These statistics are for the Stanford Executive Program classes of 2014 and 2015, with 207 respondents. But these numbers are consistent across a decade of surveying this group and other groups of participants in the Stanford Graduate School of Business (GSB) programs in (nondegree) executive education.
    - With the one exception that is noted in the text, the demographic cross-tabs of responses against age, domicile, rank/position, functional specialization, and industry make little difference to the results.
    - I have also run this survey for Stanford GSB MBA students, where "direct reports" is replaced by "peers" at their most recent

employer. Organization success is a *much* less effective motivator for this population.

4. F. J. Anscombe and Robert Aumann, "A Definition of Subjective Probability," *Annals of Mathematical Statistics* 34 (1963): 199–205.
5. For the sake of completeness, I provide formal details in the appendix, where I use the easier-to-apply mixture-space theorem approach.

4. TWO (OR THREE) HETERODOX BOOKS

1. George Akerlof and Rachel Kranton, *Identity Economics* (Princeton, NJ: Princeton University Press, 2010).
2. Dale T. Miller, *The Power of Identity Claims: How We Value and Defend the Self* (Milton Park, UK: Routledge, 2020).
3. This "step further" is hardly novel to psychologists. It is a "step further, and beyond" in terms of orthodox economics.
4. The nonlinearity inherent in stock options poses a further problem when the firm's share value is well below the options' striking price. But that is a different story; ignore this further complication here.
5. David Packard, *The HP Way. How Bill Hewlett and I Built Our Company* (New York: Collins, 1995), 135.
6. J. W. Brehm, *A Theory of Psychological Reactance* (New York: Academic Press, 1966).
7. Christina Steindl et al., "Understanding Psychological Reactance," *Zeitschrift Fur Psychologie* 223 (2015): 205–14.
8. Gabriel Burdin, Simon Halliday, and Fabio Landini, "The Hidden Benefits of Abstaining from Control," *Journal of Economic Behavior and Organization* 147 (2018): 1–12; Armin Falk and Michael Kosfeld, "The Hidden Costs of Control," *American Economic Review* 96 (2006): 1611–30. I am grateful to Sam Bowles for pointing me to this work and to the quote from Packard.

9. Roland Bénabou and Jean Tirole, "Identity, Morals and Taboos: Beliefs as Assets," *Quarterly Journal of Economics* 126 (2011): 805–55.
10. Darryl J. Bem, "Self-Perception: An Alternative Interpretation of Cognitive Dissonance Phenomena," *Psychology Review* 74, no. 3 (1967): 183–200.
11. Samuel Bowles, *The Moral Economy: Why Good Incentives Are No Substitute for Good Citizens* (New Haven, CT: Yale University Press, 2016).
12. Samuel Bowles and Herbert Gintis, *A Cooperative Species: Human Reciprocity and Its Evolution* (Princeton, NJ: Princeton University Press, 2011).
13. Bowles, *The Moral Economy*, 2.
14. Indeed, these comments were made 45 years ago. They should not be taken as serious reflections on the current state of civic culture in either country.
15. Uri Gneezy and Aldo Rustichini, "A Fine Is a Price," *Journal of Legal Studies* 29 (2000): 1–17.
16. Gary Becker, *Accounting for Tastes* (Cambridge, MA: Harvard University Press, 1998), 4–5; George Stigler and Gary Becker, "De Gustibus Non Est Disputandum," *American Economic Review* 67 (1977): 76–90.
17. Roland Bénabou and Jean Tirole, "Incentives and Prosocial Behavior," *American Economic Review* 96 (2006): 1652–78.
18. In Stigler and Becker's "De Gustibus Non Est Disputandum," the claim is made that this model is robust enough to accommodate any behavior that less orthodox models have produced. It's an interesting claim, presumably one that can be expressed formally. But, depending on how it is formalized, I'm not sure it is true. If we look at individual choices over opportunity sets for later choice, an unchanging utility function that is maximized would never produce a strict preference for a smaller opportunity set for later choice, something that is the hallmark of sophisticated choice in the style of R. Strotz, "Myopia

and Inconsistency in Dynamic Utility Maximization," *Review of Economic Studies* 23 (1955–56): 165–80. However, Becker might get away with even this, if the choice of a larger opportunity set at time t is modeled as having a deleterious effect on P_t.

5. CHOICE, PREFERENCE, AND UTILITY IN DYNAMIC CONTEXTS

1. R. Strotz, "Myopia and Inconsistency in Dynamic Utility Maximization," *Review of Economic Studies* 23 (1955–56): 165–80; David M. Kreps, "A Representation Theorem for 'Preference for Flexibility,' " *Econometrica* 47 (1979): 565–78.
2. While Strotz introduced this idea into formal economic models, the classic reference to such behavior is about as classic as can be: Odysseus, sailing past the Isle of the Sirens, had his crew lash him to the mast: he wanted to hear the Sirens' song while constrained from flinging his later self off the ship to his death.

6. SOME (SOCIAL) PSYCHOLOGY: SELF-PERCEPTION AND ATTRIBUTION THEORIES

1. This section draws heavily on the exposition of David M. Kreps, *The Motivation Toolkit* (New York: Norton, 2018), 104ff.
2. Darryl J. Bem, "Self-Perception: An Alternative Interpretation of Cognitive Dissonance Phenomena," *Psychology Review* 74, no. 3 (1967): 183–200.
3. Edward E. Jones and Keith E. Davis, "From Acts to Dispositions: The Attribution Process in Person Perception," *Advances in Experimental Social Psychology* 2 (1965): 219–66.
4. H. Tajfel and J. C. Turner, "An Integrative Theory of Intergroup Conflict," in *The Social Psychology of Intergroup Relations*, ed. S. Worchel and W. G. Austin (Monterey, CA: Brooks/Cole, 1979), 33–47.

7. INTRINSIC MOTIVATION UNDERMINED BY EXTRINSIC REWARDS?

1. See section 5 in Samuel Bowles, "Endogenous Preferences: The Cultural Consequences of Markets and Other Economic Institutions," *Journal of Economic Literature* 36 (1998): 75–111.
2. Richard M. Titmuss, *The Gift Relationship: From Human Blood to Social Policy* (1970), reissue, ed. Ann Oakley and John Aston (New York: New Press, 1997).
3. Carl Mellström and Magnus Johannesson, "Crowding Out in Blood Donation: Was Titmuss Right?" *Journal of the European Economic Association* 6 (2008): 845–63; see also Claudia Niza, Burcu Tung, and Theresa M. Marteau, "Incentivizing Blood Donation: Systematic Review and Meta-Analysis to Test Titmuss' Hypothesis," *Health Psychology* 32 (2013): 941–49, for a meta-analysis of evidence on Titmuss's hypothesis.
4. Roland Bénabou and Jean Tirole, "Intrinsic and Extrinsic Motivation," *Review of Economic Studies* 70 (2003): 489–520.
5. Roland Bénabou and Jean Tirole, "Incentives and Prosocial Behavior," *American Economic Review* 96 (2006): 1652–78.
6. For interesting field-experiment data concerning the "signaling" value of pledging to make a blood donation, see Christian Johannes Meyer and Egon Tripodi, "Image Concerns in Pledges to Give Blood: Evidence from a Field Experiment," *Journal of Economic Psychology* 87 (2021): 102434.
7. Mark R. Lepper, David Greene, and Richard E. Nisbett, "Undermining Children's Intrinsic Interest with Extrinsic Reward: A Test of the 'Overjustification' Hypothesis," *Journal of Personality and Social Psychology* 28 (1973): 129–37.
8. Does the fact that, even absent any promised reward, she is drawing not for her own pleasure but instead for a third party lead to less beautiful pictures than those she was drawing before the experiment? I don't believe that data in the experiment speak to this question.

9. What of the intermediate group? Although they were not promised a reward, one was given to them. Does the subsequent lack of a reward mean that they show less interest in drawing on their own? The data in the experiment are, I believe, inconsistent with this.

8. WHY ARE "SOCIAL PROMISES" UNSECURED?

1. Earlier versions of the story in this chapter were worked out with Bengt Holmstrom. If any merit attaches, he shares in it. If any blame attaches, it is all mine.
2. That is, if $\zeta(E, \theta) = 1$ if Kreps shows up and $= 0$ if he fails, then $\pi(E) =$ the prior probability of the event $\{\theta; \zeta(E, \theta) = 1\}$.
3. Because Kreps gets intrinsic pleasure from giving the talk, for Stiglitz to push Kreps's expected payoff to zero, he (Stiglitz) might offer an honorarium H that is less than zero. That is, Kreps pays a small fee if he shows up for the privilege of giving the talk, and he pays a larger penalty if he is a no-show.
4. Remember we're assuming that Kreps will participate when $H = 0$. Stiglitz might offer an honorarium on its own if needed to get Kreps to accept his invitation.
5. Bènabou and Tirole's stories about how the imposition of a penalty has signal-jamming implications should be taken as read.
6. To be precise, this assumes that Kreps's reduced intrinsic motivation term $\hat{B}$ doesn't depend on the size of the penalty P. The reader can work through the model if, instead, Kreps's reduced intrinsic motivation was given by a decreasing and differentiable function $P \to \hat{B}(P)$.
7. Samuel Bowles, *The Moral Economy: Why Good Incentives Are No Substitute for Good Citizens* (New Haven, CT: Yale University Press, 2016).
8. For these parameter values, Kreps appears in states $\theta \in [0, \hat{B} + H + P]$. Once Stiglitz decides to impose a positive penalty, he will choose $H + P = \$30,000$ to make the "pie" as large as

possible: even if Kreps's intrinsic motivation were to completely disappear—that is, $\hat{B} = 0$—the probability of Kreps increasing will increase, because \$30,000 is more than Kreps's initial intrinsic motivation of \$20,000.

9. See section 22.3 of David M. Kreps, *Microeconomic Foundations II: Imperfect Competition, Information, and Strategic Interaction* (Princeton, NJ: Princeton University Press, 2023), for some repeated-game-theoretic analysis of this situation when Alice and Bob take turns "trading" favors. And see T. Renee Bowen, David Kreps, and Andrzej Skrzypacz, "Rules with Discretion and Local Information," *Quarterly Journal of Economics* 128 (2013): 1273–320, for analysis of the following elaboration: Alice and Bob do not interact frequently enough for a folk-theorem-like, cooperative equilibrium between the two of them alone to emerge. But, with social enforcement—if Bob reneges on a promise to Alice, Carol and Daniel and others can punish Bob by failing to do favors for him—"trading favors with the group" can be an equilibrium. Suppose in the context of community enforcement that, when Bob can do a favor for Alice, Bob's costs and Alice's benefits are observed only by those two; all that Carol and Daniel and the rest of society know is that Bob could have done a favor for Alice and failed to do so. In such circumstances, (how) does it work for Alice to excuse Bob publicly ex ante? (How) Does it work for her to forgive him publicly ex post if he fails to do the favor?
10. There is no Cal State Ukiah, so I'm not insulting anyone here.
11. Without drifting too far from the topic, interested readers should look at the social-psychological theory known as *gift exchange* concerning the sorts of "gift" that are most effective at triggering the norm of reciprocity. I discuss gift exchange further at the end of chapter 10. Or, for a classic reference, see Alvin Gouldner, "The Norm of Reciprocity: A Preliminary Statement," *American Sociological Review* 25 (1960): 161–78, specifically the paragraph that begins "To suggest that . . ." on page 171.

9. THE QUALITY OF KREPS'S PERFORMANCE MATTERS AS WELL

1. I deal briefly with a reservation value for Stiglitz in excess of $3,331.75 in note 4.
2. Bengt Holmstrom and Paul Milgrom, "Multitask Principal-Agent Analyses: Incentive Contracts, Asset Ownership, and Job Design," *Journal of Law, Economics, and Organization* 7 (1991): 24–52.
3. If $\kappa = 0.1$, the model goes haywire. Kreps, entirely on his own—that is, with $H = P = 0$—is so unconcerned about the cost of rising quality relative to its benefit to him that, optimally, he appears with probability 1 and with a quality level of immense size. (Of course, Stiglitz is very happy with this.) Some fixing of the model is required, so that the cross partial of E with q in the cost term is, for large enough values, large enough to overcome the positive cross partial in Kreps's benefit term.
4. Suppose Stiglitz's participation constraint was that his best alternative to Kreps gives him an expected payoff of $6,000. Then the base case $H = P = 0$ won't work; Stiglitz will go with another speaker. Scenario 3 shows that with a substantial P, they can come to an arrangement meeting both participation constraints, if imposing P only lowers Kreps's intrinsic motivation by 10 percent. But this is still "socially" wasteful. One might ask whether having $H = P = 0$ and having Kreps write a check to Stiglitz regardless of appearance doesn't give an efficient outcome that meets both participation constraints. But this depends on the effect on Kreps's intrinsic incentives of being required to pay Stiglitz to be invited.
5. Of course, Stiglitz is better off at this point. With $\rho = 0.97$, splitting $H + P = \$21{,}000$ into $H = \$1{,}360$ and $P = \$19{,}640$ leaves Kreps with an expected payoff of $7.27, while Stiglitz's expected payoff is $10,788.76.
6. Holmstrom and Milgrom, "Multitask Principal-Agent Analyses."
7. This is an issue because total costs *do not* monotonically rise in this model with θ; optimizing over quality causes total cost to Kreps to fall for low values of θ.

8. That is, the average quality declines, conditional on the talk being given. If, instead, the average is computed unconditionally, assigning quality level zero to states where Kreps fails to appear, the (unconditional) average quality increases, because (in this model) any talk that is given has strictly positive quality. Compare with the first model of this chapter.

10. INTRINSIC MOTIVATION TO DO WHAT, EXACTLY?

1. The overall project was named the Stanford Project on Emerging Companies, or SPEC. The research generated several journal articles; the first of these is James N. Baron and Michael T. Hannan, "Organizational Blueprints for Success in High-Tech Start-Ups: Lessons from the Stanford Project on Emerging Companies," *California Management Review* 44 (2002): 7–36.
2. In private communication, Baron offers two other possible explanations: (1) The star model is fragile—what if the star jumps ship?—and is not easily scalable, so markets are reluctant to anoint such firms with IPO status. (2) While "stars" may discover a breakthrough product, commercialization of the product takes collaboration across the firm. The star model, which exalts the star scientist or engineer, is not necessarily the best culture for collaboration on a consummate level.
3. Deci, E. L., and R. M. Ryan, *Intrinsic Motivation and Self-Determination in Human Behavior* (New York: Plenum, 1985).
4. The hospital had two paths it could follow at this point: it could, and did, remove autonomy and authority from the senior RNs. Or it could have tried to reframe tangible incentives for the senior RNs, so that their intrinsic motivation was better aligned with the needs of the hospital; see the next section. Going down the first path had severe adverse consequences for the morale and motivation of the senior RNs. I think the second path should have been taken, but (with one exception) medical

professionals with whom I've discussed this case assure me that doing so was wholly impractical.

5. Goulder, Alvin. "The Norm of Reciprocity: A Preliminary Statement." *American Sociological Review* 25 (1960): 161–78.

11. INTERNALIZATION OF THE OTHER PARTY'S WELFARE

1. This is not meant to malign the real Joe Stiglitz, but only to keep the analysis relatively simple.
2. And consider: if Columbia puts up the money for the honorarium, Stiglitz to some extent internalizes Columbia's welfare, and Kreps does not directly internalize Columbia's welfare, then Kreps still indirectly internalizes Columbia's welfare. A "network" analysis of strong/direct and weak/indirect ties based on internalization becomes of interest.
3. See David M. Kreps, *Microeconomic Foundations II: Imperfect Competition, Information, and Strategic Interaction* (Princeton, NJ: Princeton University Press 2023), chap. 22, for formal analysis.
4. T. Renee Bowen, David Kreps, and Andrzej Skrzypacz, "Rules with Discretion and Local Information," *Quarterly Journal of Economics* 128 (2013): 1273–320.
5. Kenneth J. Arrow, "Gifts and Exchanges," *Philosophy and Public Affairs* 1 (1972): 343–62.
6. Samuel Bowles and Herbert Gintis, *A Cooperative Species: Human Reciprocity and Its Evolution* (Princeton, NJ: Princeton University Press, 2011).
7. And yet: in the formal model where both Alice and Bob have "personal-concerns" utilities and they positively internalize each others' private concerns in their "greater-concerns, overall utilities," imagine that, in their relationship, Alice does more favors for Bob and Bob does more for Alice, by virtue of each internalizing the welfare of the other. Suppose this results in an increase for each in their personal-concerns utility functions, which of

course means an even larger increase for each in their greater-concerns utilities. One must be careful in making a welfare comparison by orthodox rules. But, if each sees improvement in his or her personal-concerns utility, I'm prepared to say that this is unambiguously welfare enhancing.

12. DYNAMICS BASED ON BEM'S SELF-PERCEPTION THEORY

1. Compare with Roland Bénabou and Jean Tirole, "Identity, Morals and Taboos: Beliefs as Assets," *Quarterly Journal of Economics* 126 (2011): 805–55, for both this paragraph and the next.
2. Fryer, Roland. "Financial Incentives and Student Achievement: Evidence from Randomized Trials." *Quarterly Journal of Economics* 126 (2011): 1755–58.

   An explanation is provided by Vroom's expectancy theory (see Victor Vroom, *Work and Motivation* [New York: Wiley, 1964]), the psychological theory of motivation that economists can recognize as agency theory for boundedly rational agents: the theory is that motivation is effective when the individual understands (a) how her actions will lead to results desired by the principal (expectancy), (b) how results desired by the principal will lead to rewards for her (instrumentality), and (c) that she values those rewards (valence). In Fryer's first treatment group, expectancy is lacking: subjects know that raising their grades will lead to paid-for cell-phone bills, which they value. But they are unsure what they can do to raise grades. In the second subject group, expectancy is high: read books, get cell-phone bills paid. The link from reading books to higher grades is understood by the principal, who effectively motivates book reading.
3. Mark R. Lepper, David Greene, and Richard E. Nisbett, "Undermining Children's Intrinsic Interest with Extrinsic Reward: A Test of the 'Overjustification' Hypothesis," *Journal of Personality and Social Psychology* 28 (1973): 129–37.

4. And, to give the dark side of this, insofar as these expressive connections become stronger through time, an employer who breaks the "psychological" contract that has been formed with employees faces a severe crisis of motivation. This happened, for instance, at Beth Israel Hospital, when control was taken back from the senior RNs.
5. Readers who know about the history of graduate schools of business probably can recognize the identities of these three schools. In particular, the founding principles of school C quoted in the text are taken verbatim from the charter of a "Carnegie Institute of Technology Graduate School of Industrial Administration," which was founded in 1949.
6. H. Tajfel and J. C. Turner, "An Integrative Theory of Intergroup Conflict," in *The Social Psychology of Intergroup Relations*, ed. S. Worchel and W. G. Austin (Monterey, CA: Brooks/Cole, 1979), 33–47.

13. SHOULD ECONOMISTS MOVE IN THESE DIRECTIONS?

1. Robert M. Solow, "How Did Economics Get That Way and What Way Did It Get?" *Daedalus* 126 (1997): 39–58.
2. David M. Kreps, *Microeconomic Foundations II: Imperfect Competition, Information, and Strategic Interaction* (Princeton, NJ: Princeton University Press, 2023), 312.
3. George A. Akerlof and Rachel E. Kranton, *Identity Economics* (Princeton, NJ: Princeton University Press, 2010); Samuel Bowles, *The Moral Economy: Why Good Incentives Are No Substitute for Good Citizens* (New Haven, CT: Yale University Press, 2016).
4. Edward P. Lazear and Michael Gibbs, *Personnel Economics in Practice*, 3rd ed. (New York: Wiley, 2014).
5. James N. Baron and David M. Kreps, "Employment as an Economic and Social Relationship," in *The Handbook of Organizational Theory*, ed. R. Gibbons and D. J. Roberts (Princeton, NJ: Princeton University Press, 2013), 315–41.

6. Lazear and Gibbs, *Personnel Economics in Practice*.
7. Franklin Fisher, "Games Economists Play: A Noncooperative View," *RAND Journal of Economics* 20 (1989): 113–24.
8. In his comments to follow, the real Prof. Stiglitz observes that this was how Ken Arrow viewed general equilibrium theory. I'm happy to find myself in such august company.
9. One can only wonder how Fisher would react to the empirical work in so-called structural IO that has occurred since he composed his objections. I suspect he would see the "structural" models as too much of a straitjacket, but that is speculative.

COMMENTARY: JOSEPH STIGLITZ

1. George A. Akerlof, "The Market for 'Lemons': Quality Uncertainty and the Market Mechanism," *Quarterly Journal of Economics* 84, no. 4 (1970): 488–500. https://doi.org/10.2307/1879431
2. M. J. Sandel, *What Money Can't Buy: The Moral Limits of Markets* (New York: Farrar, Straus and Giroux, 2012).
3. Karl Polanyi, *The Great Transformation: Economic and Political Origins of Our Time* (New York: Rinehart, 1944).
4. Adam Smith, *The Theory of Moral Sentiments* (London: A. Millar, A. Kincaid and J. Bell, 1759).
5. George A. Akerlof and Rachel E. Kranton, "Economics and Identity," *Quarterly Journal of Economics* 115, no. 3 (August 2000): 715–753.
6. Max Weber, *The Protestant Ethic and the Spirit of Capitalism*, trans. Talcott Parsons. (New York: Scribner, 1905).
7. World Bank, *World Development Report 2015: Mind, Society, and Behavior* (Washington, DC: World Bank, 2015).
8. Karla Hoff and Joseph Stiglitz, "Striving for Balance in Economics: Towards a Theory of the Social Determination of Behavior," *Journal of Economic Behavior and Organization* vol. 126 (June 2016): 25–57.

COMMENTARY: ALESSANDRA CASELLA

1. Andrew Foster, Pedro Dal Bo', and Louis Putterman, "Institutions and Behavior: Experimental Evidence on the Effects of Democracy," *American Economic Review* 100 (2010): 2205–29; and Pedro Dal Bo', Andrew Foster, and Kenju Kamei, "The Democracy Effect: A Weights-Based Identification Strategy," Working Paper no. 25724 (Cambridge, MA: NBER, April 2019).

RESPONSE TO THE COMMENTS OF PROFESSORS CASELLA AND STIGLITZ

1. Daniel Kahnemann, *Thinking, Fast and Slow* (New York: Farrar, Straus and Giroux, 2011); Richard H. Thaler and Cass R. Sunstein, *Nudge: The Final Edition* (New York: Penguin, 2021).
2. Gerd Gigerenzer, Peter M. Todd, and ABC Research Group, *Simple Heuristics That Make Us Smart* (Oxford: Oxford University Press, 2000); Thomas J. Sargent, *The Conquest of American Inflation* (Princeton, NJ: Princeton University Press, 1999).
3. Robert M. Solow, "How Did Economics Get That Way and What Way Did It Get?" *Daedalus* 126 (1997): 39–58.
4. In the context of extensive-form games, self-confirming equilibria (Pierpalo Battigalli, Mario Gilli, and Cristina Molinari, "Learning and Convergence to Equilibrium in Repeated Interaction," *Richerche Economiche* 46 [1992]: 335–78; Drew Fudenberg and David K. Levine, *The Theory of Learning in Games* [Cambridge, MA: MIT Press, 1998]) is perhaps a bare beginning.
5. Chip Heath, "On the Social Psychology of Agency Relationships: Lay Theories of Motivation Overemphasize Extrinsic Incentives," *Organizational Behavior and Human Decision Processes* 78 (1999): 25–62.

6. Andrew Foster, Pedro Dal Bo', and Louis Putterman, "Institutions and Behavior: Experimental Evidence on the Effects of Democracy," *American Economic Review* 100 (2010): 2205–29; Pedro Dal Bo', Andrew Foster, and Kenju Kamei, "The Democracy Effect: A Weights-Based Identification Strategy," Working Paper no. 25724 (Cambridge, MA: NBER, April 2019).
7. Samuel Bowles, *The Moral Economy: Why Good Incentives Are No Substitute for Good Citizens* (New Haven, CT: Yale University Press, 2016).

APPENDIX: AXIOMATIC DERIVATION OF THE UTILITY MODEL OF CHAPTER 3

1. If this is new to you, you may wish to consult the subsection "The Trick" on page 105 of David M. Kreps, *Microeconomic Foundations I: Choice and Competitive Markets* (Princeton, NJ: Princeton University Press, 2013).
2. I. N. Herstein and J. Milnor, "An Axiomatic Approach to Measurable Utility," *Econometrica* 21 (1953): 291–97.
3. See Kreps, *Microeconomic Foundations I*, Chapter 5.
4. See the last steps of the proof of Proposition 5.12 in Kreps, *Microeconomic Foundations I.*

REFERENCES

Aaron, Henry J. "Distinguished Lecture on Economics in Government: Public Policy, Values, and Consciousness." *Journal of Economic Perspectives* 8 (1994): 3–21.

Akerlof, George A. "The Market for 'Lemons'." *Quarterly Journal of Economics* 84 (1970): 488–500.

Akerlof, George A., and Rachel E. Kranton. "Economics and Identity." *Quarterly Journal of Economics* 115 (2000): 715–53.

——. *Identity Economics*. Princeton, NJ: Princeton University Press, 2010.

Akerlof, George A., and Janet Yellen. "Gang Behavior, Law Enforcement, and Community Values." In *Value and Public Policy*, ed. Henry J. Aaron, Thomas E. Mann, and Timothy Taylor, 173–209. Washington, DC: Brookings Institution, 1993.

Anscombe, F. J., and Robert Aumann. "A Definition of Subjective Probability." *Annals of Mathematical Statistics* 34 (1963): 199–205.

Arrow, Kenneth J. "Gifts and Exchanges." *Philosophy and Public Affairs* 1 (1972): 343–62.

Baron, James N., and Michael T. Hannan. "Organizational Blueprints for Success in High-Tech Start-Ups: Lessons from the Stanford Project on Emerging Companies." *California Management Review* 44 (2002): 7–36.

REFERENCES

Baron, James N., and David M. Kreps. *Strategic Human Resources; Frameworks for General Managers*. New York: Wiley, 1999.

——. "Employment as an Economic and Social Relationship." In *The Handbook of Organizational Theory*, ed. R. Gibbons and D. J. Roberts, 315–41. Princeton, NJ: Princeton University Press, 2013.

Battigalli, Pierpalo, Mario Gilli, and Cristina Molinari. "Learning and Convergence to Equilibrium in Repeated Interaction." *Richerche Economiche* 46 (1992): 335–78.

Becker, Gary. *Accounting for Tastes*. Cambridge, MA: Harvard University Press, 1996.

——. "Why Every Married Couple Should Sign a Contract." *Business Week*, December 29, 1997. Available from the *Hoover Digest* (1998) under the title "Do You Swear to Love, Honor, and Cherish? Then Sign Here."

Bem, Darryl J. "Self-Perception: An Alternative Interpretation of Cognitive Dissonance Phenomena." *Psychology Review* 74, no. 3 (1967): 183–200.

Bénabou, Roland, and Jean Tirole. "Identity, Morals and Taboos: Beliefs as Assets." *Quarterly Journal of Economics* 126 (2011): 805–55.

——. "Incentives and Prosocial Behavior." *American Economic Review* 96 (2006): 1652–78.

——. "Intrinsic and Extrinsic Motivation." *Review of Economic Studies* 70 (2003): 489–520.

Bowen, T. Renee, David Kreps, and Andrzej Skrzypacz. "Rules with Discretion and Local Information." *Quarterly Journal of Economics* 128 (2013): 1273–320.

Bowles, Samuel. "Endogenous Preferences: The Cultural Consequences of Markets and Other Economic Institutions." *Journal of Economic Literature* 36 (1998): 75–111.

——. *The Moral Economy: Why Good Incentives Are No Substitute for Good Citizens*. New Haven, CT: Yale University Press, 2016.

Bowles, Samuel, and Herbert Gintis. *A Cooperative Species: Human Reciprocity and Its Evolution*. Princeton, NJ: Princeton University Press, 2011.

Bowles, Samuel, and Sandra Polanía-Reyes. "Economic Incentives and Social Preferences: Substitutes or Complements?" *Journal of Economic Literature* 50 (2012): 368–425.

Brehm, J. W. *A Theory of Psychological Reactance*. New York: Academic Press, 1966.

Burdin, Gabriel, Simon Halliday, and Fabio Landini. "The Hidden Benefits of Abstaining from Control." *Journal of Economic Behavior and Organization* 147 (2018): 1–12.

Dal Bo', Pedro, Andrew Foster, and Kenju Kamei. "The Democracy Effect: A Weights-Based Identification Strategy." Working Paper no. 25724, NBER, Cambridge, MA, April 2019.

Deci, E. L., and R. M. Ryan. *Intrinsic Motivation and Self-Determination in Human Behavior*. New York: Plenum. 1985.

Falk, Armin, and Michael Kosfeld. "The Hidden Costs of Control." *American Economic Review* 96 (2006): 1611–30.

Fehr, Ernst, and Armin Falk. "Psychological Foundations of Incentives." *European Economic Review* 46, no. 4–5 (2002): 687–724.

Fisher, Franklin. "Games Economists Play: A Noncooperative View." *RAND Journal of Economics* 20 (1989): 113–24.

Foster, Andrew, Pedro Dal Bo', and Louis Putterman. "Institutions and Behavior: Experimental Evidence on the Effects of Democracy." *American Economic Review* 100 (2010): 2205–29.

Fryer, Roland. "Financial Incentives and Student Achievement: Evidence from Randomized Trials." *Quarterly Journal of Economics* 126 (2011): 1755–58.

Fudenberg, Drew, and David K. Levine. *The Theory of Learning in Games*. Cambridge, MA: MIT Press, 1998.

Gigerenzer, Gerd, Peter M. Todd, and ABC Research Group. *Simple Heuristics That Make Us Smart*. Oxford: Oxford University Press, 2000.

Gintis, Herbert. "A Radical Analysis of Welfare Economics and Individual Development." *Quarterly Journal of Economics* 86 (1972): 572–99.

Gneezy, Uri, and Aldo Rustichini. "A Fine Is a Price." *Journal of Legal Studies* 29 (2000): 1–17.

Gouldner, Alvin. "The Norm of Reciprocity: A Preliminary Statement." *American Sociological Review* 25 (1960): 161–78.

Heath, Chip. "On the Social Psychology of Agency Relationships: Lay Theories of Motivation Overemphasize Extrinsic Incentives." *Organizational Behavior and Human Decision Processes* 78 (1999): 25–62.

Herstein, I. N., and J. Milnor. "An Axiomatic Approach to Measurable Utility." *Econometrica* 21 (1953): 291–97.

Hoff, Karla, and Joseph Stiglitz, "Striving for Balance in Economics: Towards a Theory of the Social Determination of Behavior." *Journal of Economic Behavior and Organization* 126 (2016): 25–57.

Holmstrom, Bengt, and Paul Milgrom. "Multitask Principal-Agent Analyses: Incentive Contracts, Asset Ownership, and Job Design." *Journal of Law, Economics, and Organization* 7 (1991): 24–52.

Jones, Edward E., and Keith E. Davis. "From Acts to Dispositions: The Attribution Process in Person Perception." *Advances in Experimental Social Psychology* 2 (1965): 219–66.

Kahnemann, Daniel. *Thinking, Fast and Slow*. New York: Farrar, Straus and Giroux, 2011.

Kreps, David M. *Microeconomic Foundations I: Choice and Competitive Markets*. Princeton, NJ: Princeton University Press, 2013.

——. *Microeconomic Foundations II: Imperfect Competition, Information, and Strategic Interaction*. Princeton, NJ: Princeton University Press, 2023.

——. *The Motivation Toolkit*. New York: Norton, 2018.

——. "A Representation Theorem for 'Preference for Flexibility.'" *Econometrica* 47 (1979): 565–78.

Lazear, Edward P., and Michael Gibbs. *Personnel Economics in Practice*. 3rd ed. New York: Wiley, 2014.

Lepper, Mark R., David Greene, and Richard E. Nisbett. "Undermining Children's Intrinsic Interest with Extrinsic Reward: A Test of the 'Overjustification' Hypothesis." *Journal of Personality and Social Psychology* 28 (1973): 129–37.

Mellström, Carl, and Magnus Johannesson. "Crowding Out in Blood Donation: Was Titmuss Right?" *Journal of the European Economic Association* 6 (2008): 845–63.

Meyer, Christian Johannes, and Egon Tripodi. "Image Concerns in Pledges to Give Blood: Evidence from a Field Experiment." *Journal of Economic Psychology* 87 (2021): 102434.

Miller, Dale T. *The Power of Identity Claims: How We Value and Defend the Self.* Milton Park, UK: Routledge, 2020.

Niza, Claudia, Burcu Tung, and Theresa M. Marteau. "Incentivizing Blood Donation: Systematic Review and Meta-Analysis to Test Titmuss' Hypothesis." *Health Psychology* 32 (2013): 941–49.

Packard, David. *The HP Way. How Bill Hewlett and I Built Our Company.* New York: Collins, 1995.

Polyani, Karl. *The Great Transformation: Economic and Political Origins of Our Time.* New York: Rinehart, 1944.

Sandel, Michael. *What Money Can't Buy: The Moral Limits of Markets.* New York: Farrar, Straus and Giroux, 2013.

Sargent, Thomas J. *The Conquest of American Inflation.* Princeton, NJ: Princeton University Press, 1999.

Smith, Adam. *The Theory of Moral Sentiments.* London: A Millar, A. Kincaid, and J. Bell, 1759.

Solow, Robert M. "How Did Economics Get That Way and What Way Did It Get?" *Daedalus* 126 (1997): 39–58.

Steindl, Christina, Eva Joas, Sandra Sittenthaler, Eva Traut-Mattausch, and Jeff Greenberg. "Understanding Psychological Reactance." *Zeitschrift Fur Psychologie* 223 (2015): 205–14.

Stigler, George, and Gary Becker. "De Gustibus Non Est Disputandum." *American Economic Review* 67 (1977): 76–90.

Strotz, R. "Myopia and Inconsistency in Dynamic Utility Maximization." *Review of Economic Studies* 23 (1955–56): 165–80.

Tajfel, H., and J. C. Turner. "An Integrative Theory of Intergroup Conflict." In *The Social Psychology of Intergroup Relations*, ed. S. Worchel and W. G. Austin, 33–47. Monterey, CA: Brooks/Cole, 1979.

Thaler, Richard H., and Cass R. Sunstein. *Nudge: The Final Edition.* New York: Penguin, 2021.

Titmuss, Richard M. *The Gift Relationship: From Human Blood to Social Policy.* 1970. Reissue, ed. Ann Oakley and John Aston. New York: New Press, 1997.

Vroom, Victor H. *Work and Motivation.* New York: Wiley, 1964.

Weber, Max. *The Protestant Ethic and the Spirit of Capitalism.* Translation by Talcott Parsons. New York: Scribner, 1905.

Williamson, Oliver E. *The Economic Institutions of Capitalism.* New York: Free Press, 1987.

World Bank. *World Development Report 2015: Mind, Society, and Behavior.* Washington, DC: World Bank, 2015

INDEX